Norwich The

CW00409030

The First 250 Years

Other books by Michael and Carole Blackwell

The Seventeenth Child: Memories of a Norwich Childhood 1914-1934
(with Ethel George, 2006)

By Carole Blackwell: *Tradition and Society in Turkmenistan: Gender,
Oral Culture and Song* (2001)

By Michael Blackwell: *Clinging to Grandeur: British Attitudes and Foreign
Policy in the Aftermath of the Second World War* (1993)

Norwich Theatre Royal

The First 250 Years

Michael and Carole Blackwell
with a foreword by Harriet Walter CBE

Connaught Books

First published in Great Britain in 2007 by
Connaught Books

The right of Michael and Carole Blackwell to be identified as authors of this work has been asserted by them in accordance with the Copyright, Designs and Patents Act 1988

© Copyright 2007 Michael and Carole Blackwell

All rights reserved. No part of this book may be reproduced or utilised in any form or by any means, electronic or mechanical, including photocopying, recording or by any information storage and retrieval system, without permission in writing from the publishers.

British Library Cataloguing in Publication Data
A catalogue record for this book is available from the British Library

ISBN 978-0-9557454-0-9

Cover design by Jane Goodchild
Printed in England by The Lavenham Press Ltd

Every effort has been made to contact copyright holders and obtain relevant permissions.

In memory of Tricia

Contents

List of Illustrations

Thanks for kind permission to reproduce pictures are extended to: the Norfolk Heritage Centre for pictures 4-5, 9, 16, 19, 21-22, 25, 31, 34-36, 39-41, 43-44, 48, 50, 52, 54-58, 60-64, 66, 79, 80; the Norwich Castle Museum and Art Gallery for pictures 12, 15, 17, 26-28, 42; the Norwich Theatre Royal for pictures 53, 59, 74-77, 84-85; the Parson Woodforde Society for picture 38; Archant Norfolk (formerly Eastern Counties Newspapers) for pictures 67-71; Maurice King for picture 65; Jack Bowhill for pictures 72, 82; Pat Adams for pictures 81 and 83; and Wolverhampton Art Gallery + Museums for picture 32.

Acknowledgements

We should like to thank the staffs of the Norfolk County Records Office, Norfolk Heritage Centre, Norwich Castle Museum and Art Gallery, Archant Norfolk (formerly Eastern Counties Newspapers), the archives department of the University of East Anglia Library and the British Library. Of the many people who helped us identify the documents and images we needed, we give particular thanks to Ruth Battersby Tooke, Ruth Burwood, Rosemary Dixon, Bridget Gillies, Norma Watt and Dr Clive Wilkins-Jones. We wish that Alick Williams was still with us so that we could tell him how his collection of papers was so extraordinarily useful for us. Divided between the archives at the UEA and the Heritage Centre, it represents a lifetime of work of transcribing and collecting documents related to the Theatre Royal and other local entertainment centres. For permission to use pictures in their collection we thank the Norfolk Heritage Centre, Norwich Castle Museum and Art Gallery, Archant Norfolk (formerly Eastern Counties Newspapers) and the Norwich Theatre Royal.

We also thank those who shared memories and photos of their time at the Theatre Royal notably Pat Adams, Jack Bowhill, Maurice King, Yvonne Marsh and Vivian Wall-Morris. Special thanks go to Charlotte Corbett and her students who told us about their pantomime experiences. We thank Jane Goodchild, who designed the covers of the book, Peter Hollingham, who took the back cover photograph and Nick Hunt at Lavenham Press, who laid out the book and so patiently handled all our last-minute demands. We especially thank Tony Cooper who shared his knowledge of the theatre and the arts in Norwich, rigorously edited our text and eased our way through the whole publication process.

We thank those who generously gave us their time to read our first draft and then shared their expert knowledge with us: notably Jack Bowhill, former technical director, Norwich Theatre Royal; Professor Richard Foulkes, Professor of Theatre History and Head of Department, University of Leicester and general editor of publications for the Society for Theatre Research; Frank Meeres, education and outreach officer, Norfolk Records Office and author of several books on Norfolk and Norwich history; Neville Miller, formerly theatre critic of the *Eastern Evening News*; Christopher Sexton, a good friend researching intellectual life in 18th-century Norwich and Dr Clive Wilkins-Jones, Librarian of the Norfolk Heritage Centre. We also thank two members of our family. Tim, a professional actor, was particularly helpful in advising us on how to structure the book to hold the audience's attention. Our son, Adam, who delights in exposing any weaknesses in his parents' arguments, once again gave us many valuable suggestions and ideas.

Finally, at the Norwich Theatre Royal, we thank Peter Wilson, chief executive for his support and encouragement; Jason Raper, training and education manager for his insights and special help in preparing the pictures and Mark Hazell, the theatre's marketing director, who was an invaluable source of useful contacts, an authoritative adviser on the theatre's recent history and a great help to us from the outset of this project.

Michael and Carole Blackwell

Foreword

Touring isn't popular with many actors. They dislike the disruption caused to their lives when they have to travel across the country, away from their homes and family, each week packing and unpacking a small selection of their belongings as they traipse through the land.

But actors who like touring outside London love theatres that offer comfort and decent stages. They also respond enthusiastically to cities that have a history, where the past is a tangible asset and where the audiences have knowledge, intelligence, discrimination and a hunger for the best in performance and production.

Norwich is such a city. Its audiences are discriminating, bright and educated in theatre, proud to be part of a county that has so much beautiful, unspoilt, historic scenery. Its buildings, streets and views haven't been ruined and it has a vibrant, muscular confidence which makes it truly the capital of Norfolk and of East Anglia.

This history of Norwich's wonderful Theatre Royal, encompassing the lives of so many who have devoted their professional careers to it, does a great service. Through the depth of its research it brings the past to life most meticulously. It is truly a labour of love and I hope that as you read it you will be able to taste a flavour of how the lives of a great theatre and of a great city add richness to one another.

Harriet Walter, CBE

Chapter 1

Opening Night

It is 31 January 1758 and the opening night for Norwich's impressive new theatre. Let's imagine the scene.

It has been dark for over an hour. A few people, gathered near the entrance of the new theatre, are blowing on their hands and pulling their mufflers ever tighter. Under flickering oil lamps, they listen for the clattering of hooves over cobbles that will signal the arrival of the opening night audience.

The smell of horses is thick in the air, as carriages and the occasional sedan chair emerge out of the gloom and pull to a halt outside the theatre. A man in a powdered wig and soft grey velvet coat steps out of the first carriage. His blue satin waistcoat is decorated with fine gold embroidery. His companion with a fashionable beauty spot on her left cheek, wears white feathers and blue ribbons on her hair. As she steps down from the carriage, her wide-hooped skirt and flowing train spread over the path. The onlookers marvel at the magnificent silver trimming on her blue silk gown.

As the elegant people enter the new theatre, humbler folk come out. These are simply dressed young women - domestic servants who have been holding seats for hours so their employers can sit in the most desirable boxes. Now they must hurry home to make up for the work they have missed. Jostling their way past prostitutes and beggars, they head home through the ill-lit and rubbish-strewn streets around the theatre and through the market place, where a shivering young man is waiting to be freed from the stocks.

Inside the theatre, the auditorium is filling. The professionals and merchants find their seats downstairs in the pit. The men wear three-cornered hats and flat shoes with buckles, the women low-necked gowns with billowing skirts. The more soberly dressed artisans and better-off workers make their way upstairs to the gallery.

The quality folk in the boxes relax in comfortable chairs, while those in the pit and the gallery make do with backless benches. There is a distinctive smell in the air: a mix of wood and new paint and smoke from candles, oil lamps, and the open coal fires dotting the stage and auditorium. Occasionally, these smells (and the odours of infrequently-washed bodies) are diluted by something much pleasanter - the potent fragrance of oranges - as fruit sellers push their way through the aisles.

The audience, excited and impatient, chatter in their distinctive Norfolk accents. Then, at exactly 6 o'clock, the musicians begin to play, the curtains open, and an actor dressed as Shakespeare rises through a trapdoor. Standing on a pedestal, he makes a brief address to the actors, who have gathered on the stage. As he descends through the trapdoor, he lets fall a roll of paper - a prologue for the audience, which another actor picks up and reads.

After loud applause, the curtain closes to music. It reopens to reveal a fashionable chocolate house where a game of cards is just finishing. Mirabel, the dashing beau in William Congreve's *The Way of the World,* rises and addresses the man who has just beaten him: 'You are a fortunate man, Mr. Fainall.' The first play in the Theatre Royal's long history has begun.

Chapter 2

Early Drama in Norwich

From the 'mystery plays' to the 'strolling players'

The first recorded dramatic performances in Norwich were the religious mystery plays acted out in the city centre in the 15th century by the local tradesmen's guilds. These plays - which had their origins in the miracle plays of over a century earlier - had been created by members of the clergy to bring home to their congregations the key teachings of the Christian faith, particularly those embodied in the stories of Christmas and Easter. Each year, on the feast day of Corpus Christi (or later at Whitsun), the different guilds would push their wheeled and richly-decorated covered stages into Norwich's city centre and perform a cycle of plays. The mercers and drapers would begin with *The Creation of the World* and the worstead weavers would finish the day with a play about *The Holy Ghost.* Between them would be ten more plays - the one on Christmas being performed by the city's dyers, goldsmiths and saddlers and the one on Easter by the butchers, fishmongers and watermen. Despite the seriousness of the themes, the actors introduced comic characters as a way of holding the audience's attention. Cain's ploughboy and Noah's wife, for example, were always played for laughs.

A mystery play

After the Reformation, the mystery plays gave way to the morality plays most of which had a distinctly anti-Catholic message. One of the most-performed authors of morality plays was John Bale who had spent some of his teenage years in a Carmelite House in Norwich but had then gone on to Cambridge University where he became an ardent reformer. His plays harshly denounced the monastic system and its supporters and were championed by Sir Thomas Cromwell, always on the lookout for ways of solidifying public opinion against Rome. As the century wore on, plays became increasingly secular. Groups of strolling players came frequently to Norwich to perform historical dramas, tragedies and comedies - plays of the type that were perfected by Shakespeare at the century's end. Most of these troupes were small. Their members lived hand-to-mouth and travelled on foot pushing a barrow containing their rudimentary costumes and props. It was a physically-demanding life and they often appeared poor and emaciated. They did not earn much and what little they did earn was frequently spent on drink in the inns where they performed. The actors arrived in the city making as much noise as possible with drums and trumpets, or similar. They then set about selling tickets.

Typically, one of their number would have already approached the mayor or magistrates to seek permission to perform. To ease their acceptance by the city authorities, most of the companies took on the name of a noble patron. This was not always enough, though. In 1583, during a period of concern about the plague, the Earl of Worcester's Company was refused permission to perform in Norwich,

> to avoid the meetings of people this hot weather for fear of an infection, as also for that they came from an infected place.[1]

When players were refused permission to perform in the city, they sometimes set up in the Cathedral precinct (where the city authorities had no authority) or just outside the boundaries - for example, in Thorpe.

Just over a week after the Earl of Worcester's Company had been turned down, a company called Queen Elizabeth's Players performed with tragic consequences at the Red Lion Inn. The Saturday afternoon performance of the play had just started when news reached the actors that a local man by the name of Wysdon had tried to get in without paying. To make matters worse, in a struggle with the gatekeeper, the money already collected at the gate had been spilt. The play was halted. One of the actors, Bentley, costumed as a duke, rushed off stage. He pulled his sword and managed to hit Wysdon on the head with its hilt before the gatecrasher escaped into the street. Bentley chased out after him together with another actor, Singer, wearing a black doublet and a false beard and also carrying a sword. Also in pursuit was a member of the audience, Henry Browne, a servant of Sir William Paston. As they approached what is now St Stephen's Street, a bystander - obviously sympathising with the fleeing Wysdon - attacked Bentley with a stone, cutting him on the head. Witnessing this act of aggression, Browne struck the offender on the leg with his sword and then Singer waded in, cutting him down with his arming sword. The poor man, badly wounded, was carried into an adjoining house where he soon died. It was not certain who had delivered the fatal blow and there is no record of Singer or Browne being apprehended; perhaps Sir William Paston exerted some influence. It is not recorded, either, whether Wysdon made good his escape or if the performance continued as if nothing had happened.[2]

The Red Lion Inn was in Red Lion Street in the city centre. Sometime in the 19th century it became known as The Cricketers' Arms. It only closed in 1959.

During the following century the number of travelling groups grew and many of them were attracted to Norwich, which was then the second largest city in the kingdom and a centre of comparative affluence. The Red Lion Inn and the White Horse Inn near

Tombland in the city centre seem to have been the most important performance venues in the early 1600s. The King's Arms near the market place and the White Swan Inn, opposite St Peter Mancroft Church, became more important in the early 1700s. (In 1716, the White Swan tried to distinguish itself from its rivals by declaring that its plays were for the 'Quality, gentry and others'.) But there were many other venues that hosted other types of performers and there were all sorts of shows on offer: travelling freak shows (including a two-headed baby, a monstrous child, a handless woman showing 'divers work with her feet' and the hairy man Francis Owen); animal shows (including baboons, bears, dancing horses, elephants and tigers); waxworks; jugglers and acrobats. In 1607, Sir Edward Coke, one of Norfolk's richest and most influential men, (he was then serving as the Chief Justice of the Court of Common Pleas), complained about how the county was troubled with stage players.[3] Court records show that in 1616 and 1620 several people were brought before the court for some kind of involvement in stage plays.[4] And, in 1623, the Privy Council, obviously responding to complaints raised by the Norwich authorities, wrote to the mayor granting him authorisation to forbid players, tumblers, dancers and that type of 'vagrant and licentious rabble'.[5]

It was only after the outbreak of the Civil War in 1642 - and particularly after the coming to power of the Puritan Oliver Cromwell as Lord Protector in 1653 - that the Norwich authorities at last succeeded in their efforts to control the numbers of performers in the city. The Puritan Parliament legislated to define all actors as rogues and vagabonds, liable to be whipped or imprisoned if they exercised their vocation. Parliament also required the demolition of stages and theatre set-ups round the country and even decreed fines of five shillings for every person caught watching a theatre performance. While Norwich was never wholeheartedly behind Cromwell and the revolution, the city authorities implemented the legislation, even preventing the traditional guild or feast-day processions where local people, many in costume, marched through the streets making music and carrying banners and model dragons. These were attacked for being 'popish, idolatrous, superstitious and unruly'.[6]

Nell Gwynn, one of the first women to appear on stage and a mistress of Charles II

After the restoration of the monarchy in 1660, pressures on performers eased. Charles II encouraged the opening of new theatres in London and was an enthusiastic patron. Women were allowed on the stage for the first time and the new plays, in a marked break from the Puritan years, were often quite bawdy. However, while the king supported the opening of new theatres in Westminster - and would sometimes license a company of actors to tour - he was reluctant to license the establishment of permanent theatres elsewhere in the country. Theatre still had many opponents. The king and the political authorities, fearing that plays might carry seditious messages, were reluctant to license spaces where audiences could gather to witness potentially-subversive productions. And local authorities throughout the country remained wary of any occasion that brought large groups of people together because of the risk of public disorder that they brought. In addition, many religious authorities still believed that theatrical performances encouraged immorality. Finally, some local authorities and employers feared that theatres led to time wasting and took ordinary people away from their labours. For these reasons, the Puritan anti-theatre legislation was not removed from the statute books and actors outside the permitted theatres in London could still fall foul of local authorities and be brought before the courts as vagrants.

Consequently, in the first decades after the Restoration, large cities such as Norwich could not establish resident theatre companies of their own and still relied on strolling players moving from one town to another. However, during the summer months, Norwich sometimes received troupes of somewhat better-off London-based actors who toured the country when the London theatres were closed. The importance of Norwich is implied in the prologue to Sir George Etherege's popular 1664 play, *The Comical Revenge*:

> We and Our comedies
> Must trip to Norwich or for Ireland go

Strolling players performing in a barn

By 1669, performing groups visiting Norwich had become so numerous that the authorities feared that they were having a negative impact on the city's economy. In December of that year, the mayor and aldermen sent the city recorder, Thomas Corie, to meet Lord Arlington, who was then Secretary of State at Charles II's court. He met him in Thetford (presumably at his near-by country home of Euston Hall) and gave him a letter from the mayor requesting that Arlington use his good services with the king 'to obteyne an order to prevent ye actinge of stage plaies in ye City'.

The letter complained that the frequent visits of stage and puppet players diverted 'the meaner sort of people' from their work in the manufactories. (Since performances rarely began after 6 o'clock, workers had to leave their employment early to attend.) The strolling players, the city authorities claimed, 'drain too much money from the inhabitants' and Norwich 'is being daily impoverished by decay of trade and the charge of maintaining the poor'. On

Lord Arlington

Christmas Eve, Corie followed up with a letter to Arlington's secretary, Sir Joseph Williamson, asking him if he could help hasten action as they expected players to return within 14 days. He wrote again on 5 January (giving the prevalence of smallpox in the city as an added reason for action) and again before the end of the month. The king finally gave a positive response in mid-February. To the mayor's relief, he authorised the city authorities 'to determine the time during which the said players shall stay in the city, and they are to remain no longer, any license from us or the Master of the Revels notwithstanding'.[7] It is interesting to note that this complaint was based on financial considerations and not on fears of immorality or breakdown in public order.

> **The Master of Revels** was a deputy to the Lord Chamberlain who was in charge of organising theatrical entertainment at Court, auditioning troupes and selecting (and often censoring) plays. His remit grew to being responsible for the licensing of all theatres and all theatre groups in the country including the bands of strolling players.

Relationships between players and local authorities were still tense at the beginning of the 18th century. The fears of the local authorities about political sedition, immorality and adverse economic impact remained the same. John Wesley summed up these last two concerns:

> most of the present stage entertainments sap the foundation of all religion, as they naturally tend to efface all traces of piety and seriousness out of the minds of men; but as they are peculiarly hurtful to a trading city, giving a wrong turn to youth especially, gay, trifling, and directly opposite to the spirit of industry and close application to business; and, as drinking and debauchery of every kind are constant attendants on these entertainments, with indolence, effeminacy, and idleness, which affect trade in an high degree.[8]

Perhaps the main reason, though, that the Norwich authorities were wary of theatrical performances was the potential for public disorder in their rapidly-growing city. Improving child-survival rates were increasing the number of potentially-unruly young people while the influx of immigrants from the depressed surrounding villages increased the number of ill-housed hungry unemployed. In the days before the establishment of a police force, the authorities could not respond quickly to a crowd that got out of control. They were particularly concerned about the cheaper forms of entertainment such as puppet shows that attracted a rough crowd to drinking establishments. There was considerably less concern about musical performances and theatre companies often resorted to obtaining a license for some kind of musical concert at which they performed a play free of charge between two short pieces of music. This was a practice sometimes followed by the Theatre Royal in its early years.

Norwich's first resident companies

But try as they may, local governments could not suppress the popular support for theatrical performance, particularly since much of this support came from the local gentry and the politically-influential merchants and middle classes. In fact, by the 1730s, several troupes had established a headquarters in one town or city and limited their touring to the towns and villages of the region. This was the case in Norwich where two companies - the Duke of Norfolk's Company and the Duke of Grafton's Servants - competed throughout the East Anglian region. Ultimately, the latter company prevailed and transformed itself into the Norwich Company of Comedians that was to become the Theatre Royal's stock company from its opening until well into the 19th century.

The Duke of Grafton

Local and national authorities fretted about the development of more permanent local theatre groups and, in response to their concerns, Parliament passed a new Licensing Act in 1737. The act confirmed earlier legislation that any actors performing without the king's patent or chamberlain's license would be doing so illegally and could be deemed rogues or vagabonds. Since patents and licenses were only issued for Westminster and wherever the king happened to be; this meant that any performances in Norwich were, technically, against the law. However, the act seems to have made little impact in the city; actors continued to perform and the authorities only intervened when a performance led to a breach of the peace or triggered complaints. In the early 1700s there were at least seven Norwich locations that were used regularly for the performance of plays.

The Duke of Grafton, interestingly, married Isabella the daughter of Lord Arlington, mentioned earlier. The king arranged the marriage when they were only children. They married when Grafton was 16 years old and Isabella only 12. They moved to Euston Hall, three miles from Thetford, six years later. At the time, the theatre company was performing under his patronage, he was serving as Lord Chamberlain.

The performing space was by this time inside the inn rather than in a courtyard. The construction work to form the space was not always of the highest quality. At the Angel, near the market place in 1699, a crowded gallery fell during a performance, killing one girl and injuring several others. After it was reconstructed, the manager issued a notice reassuring people that:

> The Play House at The Angel in the Market Place being new built by Mr Starling the Carpenter, for the reception of Gentlemen, Ladies and others; This is to give notice that such care is taken by the said Mr Starling for the Strength and security of the Galleries, etc., that there will be no reason to fear any Danger, as has been maliciously insinuated: and he, the said Mr Starling, will give further Satisfaction to any person or persons who desire it.[9]

The reference to 'malicious insinuations' probably points to vigorous competition between the different performance venues.

Attending a play was not always a comfortable experience. Most venues had only common benches for the spectators to sit on with a few better seats in boxes next to the stage, or, in some cases, on chairs placed directly on the stage. Thus the better-off patrons could get closer to the action, be seen themselves and, importantly, keep warmer in the winter. In a *Norwich Gazette* of 1725 one of the theatres reassured patrons that:

> The pit is lined, and there are boxes on the stage for the better reception of gentlemen and ladies. There will be two fires kept on the stage during the time of performance that the room may be warm.[10]

A few years later, in 1734, the Red Lion announced: 'That the Gentry may not be incommoded with Cold, there are Contrivances to keep the House Warm.'

It was very important to attract the gentry to the theatre; if they attended, then other ranks of society would follow. Socially-mixed audiences, though, brought their own problems as the players had to try to appeal to the better-educated and more-refined 'quality' audience as well as to the simpler folk in the gallery who were thought to prefer buffoonery and bellowing. Spectators sitting in the highest-priced seats on the stage often caused problems for the performers. There are frequent reports of performances being hampered by audience members conversing with each other across the stage, moving their chairs around or walking about during the course of the play. The Norwich theatres tried all approaches over the years to limit the number of people on the stage: from the peremptory notices - 'None admitted on the stage!' - to the obsequious - '... hope the Gentlemen and Ladies not take ill, if no one can be admitted on the stage, more than the seats will contain.' The inconveniences were well illustrated by an accident reported during a performance at the White Swan in 1725. Mrs Bedingfield wrote to a friend that when a stage trapdoor opened, four people fell in: 'one a particular man, who was high-sheriff last year, fell upon a pretty woman, and liked his situation so well, that they could not get him out.'[11]

Acting companies had to share these Norwich locations with many other types of performers. During the early 1700s, all kinds of show people passed through the city. There were companies whose members were closer to clowns than bona-fide actors. They sometimes performed short farces known as 'drolls'. There were other companies that performed song medleys or extracts from plays and operas. And then there were acrobats, conjurers, waxworks, freak shows, boxing competitions and puppeteers. Puppet plays were particularly popular during this period. In the 1740 Christmas season alone, there were three puppet shows on in the city and it was reported that, at one of the locations, 100 people per night were being turned away.[12]

By 1731, the White Swan Inn - opposite the site of the present Theatre Royal - had become the best equipped of all the performing spaces. It had a decent-sized stage, a pit for the musicians and two galleries. It was in that year that the Norwich Company of Comedians made it their headquarters and stopped their performances at the King's Arms.

The company began offering programmes not just for a few days but for seasons stretching over several weeks. As it established itself and brought in increasing revenues for the inn, improvements were made that transformed the space into a proper theatre.

Major renovations were undertaken in 1739 including the erection of 'commodious boxes ... for the ladies' (these were big enough for them to enter with their generously-proportioned dresses) and the painting of new scenery and backdrops by the famous French scene painter, John Devoto, who had been brought to Norwich for the occasion. (He did not complete his work on time for the planned opening night, which had to be put back a day because 'the Paintings would scarcely be dry before that Time'.)[13] More improvements were made in 1742 when it was said that the 'White Swan Play-House is finished up so well, as to make it capable of entertaining the finest Musical Hands for Concerts, as well as Playing'. For the spectators' winter comfort the playhouse was 'ceiled, and made very warm'. The final round of improvements to the White Swan before the opening of Thomas Ivory's new theatre came in 1747 in preparation for the visit

The stage trapdoor

of one of the country's most-renowned actors, Charles Macklin. For the audience's comfort the house was 'alter'd and fitted up ... in a commodious and theatrical manner'. The renovations may well have included the construction of upper-level boxes, because there is a reference to these in 1749.[14]

The White Swan Inn 1752

Charles Macklin

Macklin had a fiery temper and some 12 years before his Norwich debut he had killed a fellow actor in the green room at Drury Lane. He had taken exception to the fact that the unfortunate Mr Hallam had put on the wig that he (Macklin) had worn the night before. An argument ensued and Macklin thrust his stick in Hallam's eye fatally wounding him. He was convicted of manslaughter at the Old Bailey but soon resumed his acting career. He carried on acting until 1789, when he was nearly 90. He went on stage to play Shylock but lasted for only a few minutes before apologising to the audience for his wandering memory and retired for good. He died aged 98.

Macklin was a 'larger-than-life' character whose presence filled the stage, particularly in his rendition of Shylock in *The Merchant of Venice*. In Norwich, he played Macbeth. His coming to the city was a sign that it was establishing for itself an enviable reputation as a centre for theatre excellence and the inn upped the ticket prices to help defray the costs of his fee and of the new scenes (painted by the 'best hands in London') and of the new 'rich and elegant costumes'.

During Macklin's season, ticket prices were raised by 50 per cent.

Ticket prices during Macklin's Norwich season 1747		
Location	Price	2007 equivalent (inflation adjusted)
Boxes	3s. 0d.	£20
Pit	2s. 6d.	£17
Lower Gallery	1s. 6d.	£10
Upper Gallery	1s. 0d.	£7

The Norwich Company of Comedians was formed of a core of professional actors with experience on the London stage together with a few locally-recruited members. Acting was a more demanding profession then than it is today with companies generally performing more than one play in an evening and several during the course of a week. When recruiting new players, managers inquired not only about what parts they had played but the number of 'lengths' they could master nightly. A length was 42 lines and often actors were given only two or three days to learn parts that were several lengths long. Life was also hard, because even established groups spent many weeks a year on the road staying in rudimentary accommodation. And because of the absence of established ticket offices, actors not only had to work on preparing and performing plays, but also to spend many hours helping the playbill distributors by taking playbills to shops and stalls as well as hawking tickets.

Tate Wilkinson, who had spent time acting in Norwich, recalled how the company travelled with horses pulling their six-ton wagons of props and effects, accompanied by a band of scruffy-looking, travel-stained, stage-keepers, property men, lamplighters and bill-stickers. 'For the towns on the circuit,' he said, 'their arrival was heralded by a fanfare

Charles Macklin as Shylock

of trumpets and drums - one of the great events of the year.[15]   On one occasion the company got stuck in the muddy wetlands of Breydon on the approach to Great Yarmouth.[16]

The Norwich Company generally played in Norwich between January and April or May. They then went on a tour of the East Anglian circuit visiting such important towns as Colchester, Ipswich, King's Lynn, Lowestoft and Great Yarmouth but also visiting much smaller ones too, such as Beccles, Swaffham and North Walsham. If the actors were lucky, they could count on a regular salary; otherwise they received an unpredictable share of the profits. Regular actors in the Norwich Company were probably miffed when stars were brought in from London, because the regulars lost the chance of starring roles and found their pay packets lighter.

Shakespeare was at the heart of the Norwich Company's repertoire in the early 18th century. Sixteen Shakespeare plays were performed (mostly several times) between 1720 and 1750 together with some Shakespearian adaptations. Tragedies were more popular than the comedies with *Macbeth* being the most popular with 12 productions followed by *King Lear* and *Timon of Athens*. The company also performed contemporary plays, often soon after their London premieres. In 1728, John Gay's *The Beggar's Opera* opened to acclaim in London in the January and then in Norwich in the April. In 1743, Henry Fielding's *The Wedding Day* opened in Norwich after it had been 'acted at London this winter with great applause'. The company also performed favourites of the period such as George Farquhar's *The Beaux Stratagem* and translations of some foreign-language classics such as Moliere's *Les Fourberies de Scapin* in 1741.

By the mid-18th century, the Norwich Company of Comedians had become a professional and well-paid company having a substantial following in Norwich and the region. It seemed clear that the city could support a larger and better-equipped theatre than the White Swan. Such a theatre would satisfy local demand for dramatic performances and promise the entrepreneur who built it a good return on his investment. In 1757, a man stepped forward to take on this challenge. The theatre he built became the Norwich Theatre Royal.

Chapter 3

1758 - 1768: The First Decade

Choosing a site for the theatre

The building that was to become the Norwich Theatre Royal was built in Chapel Field, an area tucked inside the old city wall and on the western side of the city centre. In the 13th century, a large church had been raised there and over the years a complex of buildings used for the education and accommodation of priests and for chantries had been added. In the early 16th century, during the period of Henry VIII's Dissolution of the Monasteries, the church and many of the associated buildings were demolished. (During this period, Norwich lost 22 medieval churches and several chapels, chantries and hospitals.) The buildings left on the site passed into the hands of the Cornwallis family and, in 1573, they were consolidated and converted into a townhouse with associated stables and gardens. The house became known as *Chapel in the Field House*. In 1609, the corporation of Norwich granted the lease of the house (*Chapply Field House*) to city MP, Sir Henry Hobart, in recognition of his services to the city and following his appointment as Attorney-General.

Hobart acquired more of the surrounding land but, from 1616, he spent decreasing amounts of time in this city property as he devoted his efforts to the rebuilding of his new country seat - Blickling Hall. The house in Chapel Field remained with the Hobarts for several generations but they used it only occasionally and took to leasing out all or parts of it. By the 18th century it had become a centre for the Whig Party during election times and provided assembly rooms for balls and parties. (The surrounding grounds became known as the venue for more dubious encounters; for instance, in 1733, three naked men were apprehended there and brought before the court.)

Sir Henry Hobart

It was a popular and crowded place and a group of aldermen wanted to develop it as a facility for the city (they no doubt also felt that it would be a good private investment). In 1753, seven of them succeeded in persuading the latest Hobart owner - by then ennobled as the Earl of Buckingham - to sell them a 500-year lease on the property. The following year they were joined by 24 other men 'of position and influence' in signing a deed of covenant setting themselves up as the proprietors of a company that would develop the site for a *House for Assemblies*, a place not only for meetings, but also for theatre and entertainments such as card playing and bowls. They engaged Norwich's most successful architect and builder, Thomas Ivory. He completed the conversion of the old buildings in about a year and the new Assembly House was opened in 1755.

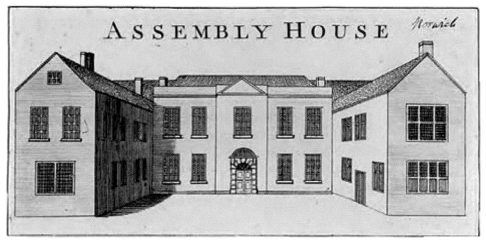

The Assembly House completed 1755

The lease agreement dated 1 April 1757 granting Thomas Ivory the right to erect a playhouse

Over the years this building has survived floods and fires and managed to retain much of its original character and still sits at the heart of Norwich's cultural life. The renovations, however, turned out to be more costly than the proprietors had bargained for and so the inclusion of a theatre on the site was dropped from the original plans.

Thomas Ivory thought that he could succeed in financing and building a theatre himself. The proprietors, therefore, agreed to lease him a plot of land of just over 6000 square feet beside the Assembly House. The lease was for 400 years at a rent of £30 per year. To raise the £600 he needed for the project, Ivory persuaded a group of local gentlemen, mostly local lawyers and merchants, to invest £20 each.[17] It was agreed that they would pay the money in instalments: £5 when the foundation was laid, £10 when the building was covered in and the remaining £5 when the work was completed. In return, he promised to pay them a yearly dividend and grant them permanent free entrance to the theatre. In the early spring of 1757, with the financing arranged, Thomas Ivory began work on what was to become the Theatre Royal.

It seems that Ivory consulted with Sir James Burroughs, Master of Gonville and Caius College, Cambridge, on the design of the building, but there is no evidence of how much (if anything at all) Burroughs contributed. The design was not entirely original anyway as it was a long brick edifice modelled on London's Drury Lane Theatre.

> **Thomas Ivory's Norfolk legacy**
> There are numerous Thomas Ivory buildings in the county. In Norwich, besides the Assembly Rooms, the most important are St Helen's House in the grounds of the Great Hospital (1752), the Octagon Chapel in Colegate (1756) and the Georgian terrace in Surrey Street (c 1761)

Building the theatre

Work on the building proceeded rapidly. After about eight months, the *Norwich Mercury* reported with some excitement:

> we are informed that the new theatre now building by Mr Ivory (for plays and musical entertainments) under the direction of Mr Collins will not only be the most convenient, but the best calculated, both for sight and sound, of any theatre in Europe; and that several absurdities, and shocking improprieties, common to the theatres will be avoided, from the construction of the stage, and the disposition of the decorations.[18]

There was much curiosity among the local population and, through the pages of the *Mercury*, Ivory had to implore them to stop popping in to see how the work was proceeding:

> to all gentlemen and ladies: the proprietor of the new theatre humbly requests that no gentlemen or ladies would desire admittance till the same is quite finished; as the business they are engaged in there, will receive great injury and be much incommoded thereby; and as he has given this public notice, hope no gentlemen or ladies will give themselves of going for that purpose till the house is open, or take it amiss in case of refusal of admittance.[19]

As the building was going up, Ivory persuaded the Norwich Company of Comedians to move from the White Swan Inn to the new theatre. Ivory purchased all the troupe's scenery and backdrops, costumes and effects and the various rights to perform in other theatres on the company's circuit. He recruited other necessary staff, notably doorkeepers and box keepers, check collectors, wardrobe staff, a morning porter, a carpenter and a hairdresser.[20] He also sold the rights to sell oranges in the theatre. Thus all would be ready to roll as soon as building work was completed. It was finished by the end of January 1758 and on the 28th of that month, the *Norwich Mercury* announced:

> The Grand and Magnificent Theatre in this City, which is now finished, and to be open'd on Tuesday the 31st of this Instant January, is allow'd by all Conniseurs and Judges, to be the most perfect and compleat Structure of the kind in this Kingdom. It is most admirably constructed for seeing and hearing; the Stage is large and lofty; and the Scenes so highly finish'd and executed, by the late ingenious Mr Collins, that they are accounted far superior to any of the kind.

Apparently, there were rumours in the city that the large galleries could collapse under the weight of a full audience. Ivory, therefore, had the *Mercury* include in the same issue an affidavit signed by three bricklayers and three carpenters stating that the building was entirely safe

> and that it is impossible for any part of the building to be mov'd by any weight or number of persons that it can possibly contain.[21]

Thomas Ivory's new theatre completed in 1758

Opening night

Once the theatre was finished it was called 'The New Theatre near Chapel Field' and playbills went up all over the city advertising the opening night for 31 January 1758. On the bill were two well-known plays of the time: William Congreve's comedy *The Way of the World* and Henry Fielding's farce *The Mock Doctor* (Ivory had, in fact, intended to open with Shakespeare's *Romeo and Juliet* but had to postpone this 'the procession not being completed, nor the music properly adapted'.)[22] Dancing performances between the acts were promised. Tickets were advertised with prices ranging from three shillings for the best seats to sixpence in the gallery. These were sold at several locations round the theatre.

When the curtains parted at 6 o'clock, the audience saw an actor dressed as Shakespeare rise up through a trapdoor reclining on a pedestal, a replica of the playwright's tomb. He delivered a short address to actors (the words of which have, unfortunately, been lost) and then, as he descended, let fall a roll of paper, a prologue for the audience, which was taken up and read by one of the Norwich Company of Comedians, Mr McClellan:

The Prologue read by Mr McClellan on Opening Night

When first the Muses breath'd Dramatic
Lays
Their dress was rude, their Stage the
Publick ways
Their song unpolish'd, dissonant and loud,
To catch the Attention of th' unpolish'd
crowd;
But tho' thus barb'rous, rude, deform'd
and mean,
Yet some were found to patronize 'em
then,
Some gen'rous Breasts, whose judgment
cou'd forsee
What the Young Art in length of Time
might be.
Then like th' Approaches of the Morning
light,
The Stage improv'd, and by Degrees grew
bright
Because the Mirror, which displays the
Charms
Of Virtue, drest in her most lovely forms;
Where erring mortals might distinctly see,
What they shou'd not, and what they
ought to be
Hence Shakespeare, Jonson, Dryden chose
the Stage
At once to please and to reform the Age;
The tender Passions of the Soul to move
And shew the judgments due to perjur'd
Love;
To curb the wild Pursuits of Thoughtless
Youth
And gently lead 'em to the Paths of Truth;
To shew that Merit tho' distrest may shine,
(Distresses tend to prove it more Divine!)
That still the Virtuous Man alone is Great
Since Virtue only mocks the frowns of
Fate.
In this have we assumed Theatric Dress,
And hence we drew our Prospect of Success
Hence too, presume We boldly to appear

Before this kind Assemblage circled here ;
Who many years have frank Indulgence
shewn,
And deign'd to call this company their own
Which favour still we'll struggle to deserve,
Ne'er from the Path of Grateful Duty
swerve,
But Toil in cheerful Heart and willing
Nerve.
May Peace and Plenty thro' this City flow,
And all the Blessings Future can bestow;
Sick Trade revive, and drooping
Commerce smile,
Commerce, the Boast and Bulwark of our
Isle
This ample fabrick rais'd at large expense
We hope will meet with ample
Recompence
Or Else (as Archer says) did fair Machine
Fall like the Edistone, at once, Souse in[a].
But that's a needless fear-you'll ne'er allow
Us to be Sufferers for pleasing you.
'Tis True
No Garricks, Barrys,[b] We pretend to be,
Such We presume you'll not expect to see,
Nor search for Cibber, Pritchard or yet
Bellamy[c]
For our whole Corps this short Conclusion
draws,
Our End is gain'd in gaining your
Applause;
Indulg'd with which no Study will seem
hard,
Your Servants We, and You our Special
Guard!
Be it our Sphere to Labour, Yours to
Reward

[a] A reference to the fall of the Eddystone
lighthouse in 1703
[b] 18th-century actors
[c] 18th-century playwrights

Then the first play of the evening began, Congreve's *The Way of the World*. This comedy of manners - first performed a half-century earlier - demands a sophisticated audience. The play has a complicated structure of plot and subplots. It features members of the gentle classes and relies for its impact on the wittiness and well-timed delivery of the text. While certainly a classic, the play's demanding nature has meant that it has not been a favourite with many audiences. Perhaps the choice of this play sent a signal that the new theatre was not going to imitate the fare of the smaller theatres in the city, but was providing for Norwich's more cultivated classes. The second play was *The Mock Doctor, or the Dumb Lady Cur'd,* Henry Fielding's adaptation of Moliere's *Le Médecin Malgré Lui*. While this was definitely a farce and much less demanding than Congreve, it was a piece of higher quality than most of the farces that had made up the bill in previous locations where the Norwich Company had performed.

The theatre's first decade

The theatre experience of this opening night was different in numerous ways from the theatre experience at the beginning of the 21st century. The picture below of an 18th-century performance in progress is instructive. Smoking candles provide the only stage lighting and boxes are on the stage itself. The picture reveals what the contemporary spectator would likely see as exaggerated body language on the part of the actors. In the days before voice amplification, actors not only had to speak in loud declamatory style but also had to use an established vocabulary of hand signs and body postures to represent their emotions. The picture also shows how audience members used to talk among themselves, thereby making it even harder to hear the actors. Georgian audiences tended to watch plays as their descendants watch a sporting fixture today, feeling no constraint on carrying on a conversation or a running commentary on the spectacle nor, indeed, of shouting complaints or encouragement to the performers.

One other major difference was the length of the programme. The formal style of acting of the 18th century made plays quicker to perform than with today's more natural acting styles. Nevertheless, with two plays and numerous musical and dance interludes, programmes would often take five or more hours to

A Georgian theatre performance

complete, meaning that patrons who had arrived at 6 o'clock would not be able to leave until 11 o'clock or later if they wanted to stay till the end. According to the *Mercury*, the opening night was a great success with the 'very numerous genteel and polite audience'.[23]

Ivory and his backers must have been pleased with the success of the theatre, but not totally relaxed. Like the other provincial permanent theatre groups, Ivory had the goodwill of the local magistrates and the support of a good part of the city's better-heeled who welcomed the new opportunities for sociability and amusement that the theatre provided. Technically, though, the theatre operation was illegal since it flouted the Licensing Act of 1737. Perhaps Ivory feared that the size of his new theatre would attract attention from the national authorities in London and that he had been too bold in calling his building a 'theatre' in light of the licensing law. To play it safe, in the year following the opening, he dropped the title of the *New Theatre near Chapel Field* and renamed the building *The Grand Concert Hall*. The playbills were redrafted accordingly to advertise concerts of music with plays presented free as interludes. No one was fooled, of course, but this nod towards the letter of the law does seem to have protected the theatre from an early closure or court case. This was the time when 'burlettas' came into fashion. These were originally comic operettas, but in the mid-18th century the word was used in a very elastic way to describe any piece that included songs or music. Therefore, if a theatre management felt under pressure, a farce or a more serious play could be performed - and as long as it had some music added to it - it could be called a 'burletta'.

During the theatre's opening decade, the company presented performances in a wide variety of genres including tragedies, comedies, farces, ballad and comic operas, pantomimes, masques and burlettas. Shakespeare remained a staple part of the company's stock of plays but often in bowdlerised and adapted forms. In March 1758, for example, the manager announced that the delayed presentation of *Romeo and Juliet* was now in rehearsal by the company in a revised version:

> To the public: As it has been remarked by some persons that the favourite play of *Romeo and Juliet* would give much more satisfaction to the audience in general if it ended happily, accordingly it has been entirely alter'd, the 5th set (made almost a new one) saving their lives, and the lives of every virtuous unoffending character in the play is [sic] preserved also (except Mercutio) & rewarded. All this, too, is brought about by nothing even bordering upon the miraculous but by fair and natural and far from improbable means. Life in all places should never fail reward for the encouragement of others to pursue it; and vice crush'd to occasion abhorrence.[24]

Performing Shakespeare

The thought of performing Romeo and Juliet with a happy ending seems nonsensical today but in the late 18th century and on into the 19th the Norwich Company of Comedians often performed feel-good versions of Shakespeare's tragedies. Prominent in its repertoire was Tate's adaptation of King Lear in which Cordelia stayed alive to live happily ever after with her father. The company also played a lighter version of Macbeth and in 1761 the theatre advertised a production of the play in which Signior Rossignole from Naples would perform his imitations of birds - from the wren to the raven - followed by a quartetto of his own composition on a violin without any strings. The management assured the public that Macbeth had been very much altered 'in order to allay fears of ladies who might be alarmed by the thunder and lightning in the play'.

The company sometimes presented plays that provided a visual representation of big stories in the news. For example, in April 1762, as British forces approached the climax of their battles with the French in North America, the company presented *The French Drubb'd or The English Tars in America,* presumably to patriotic applause. This followed several performances of Shakespeare's *Henry V*, which had first been announced on the playbills as *King Henry Vth or the Conquest of France by the English.*

During this early period of the theatre's history, the management were ever conscious of the need to make sure that the gentlemen and high social-status families of the city became regular attenders. The tone of the theatre's communications to these families was generally ingratiating. In March 1766, however, the management felt it had to confront several such families that had taken to booking out entire boxes and then arriving with nowhere near enough people in their party to fill the available seats. This - the management explained - excluded 'several other ladies and gentlemen when there had been sufficient room for them' and caused 'numerous Disappointments and Inconveniences'. The solution was to move to the system already being applied in the London theatres, where tickets had to be purchased in advance for a specific number of seats within a box. Claiming that it was acting with 'the approbation and at the desire of several of the principal ladies and gentlemen of Norwich', the management 'humbly requested' offenders to comply with the new system.[25]

The less gentle parts of the audience in the pit and the galleries also posed their problems. One writer looked back on the 1767 season and wrote that there were two classes of people who attended the theatre that were 'pests'.

> Some, tho' not able to read, take a sovereign pleasure in openly criticising the performers, others expose their ignorance in ludicrous observations, remarks on the audience, and shifting from one part of the house to the other.[26]

On the tenth anniversary of his theatre building, despite the problems, Ivory was able to look back with some satisfaction. Above all, he had survived the sometimes 'all-too-difficult' legal environment unscathed. His theatre company was well established and numbered among it some accomplished performers. The audiences, while not always large or well disciplined, were consistently good enough to keep the operation viable and generally profitable. Later that year, Ivory received news from London that caused great celebrations and promised to raise the theatre to new levels of achievement.

Norwich in 1783

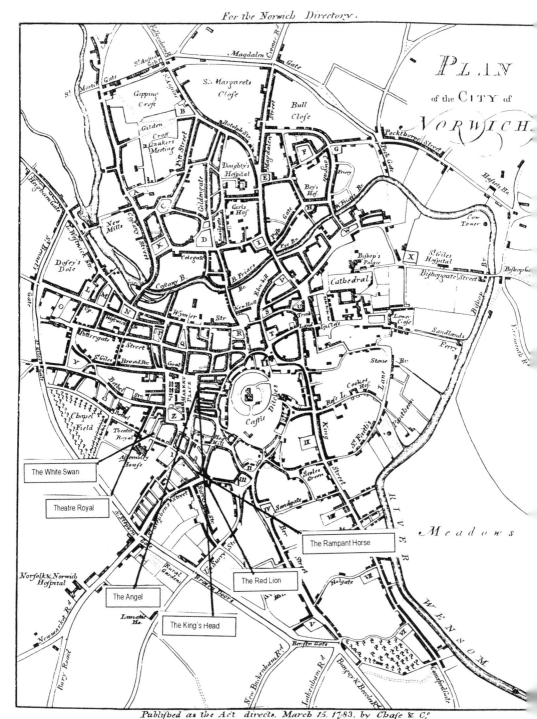

The White Swan

Theatre Royal

Norfolk & Norwich Hospital

The Angel

The King's Head

The Rampant Horse

The Red Lion

Chapter 4

1768 - 1825: The Georgian Period

Representations made to Parliament in 1767 to legalise theatres outside London finally bore fruit and acts were passed that empowered the Lord Chamberlain to grant licenses for the performance of stage plays in Edinburgh in 1767 followed by Bath and Norwich the following year. The Norwich Act was given the Royal Assent on 8 March 1768[27] and the license was issued on the 17th of that month, just a few days later than the one issued for Bath. Thus Norwich narrowly missed out on the honour of being the first royally-sanctioned provincial theatre in England. There was relief and celebration when the news reached Norwich. The *Norwich Mercury* commented:

> our regular and elegant theatre which has hitherto been honor'd by the approbation and countenance of the sensible and polite will now also happily enjoy the sanction and protection of our laws.[28]

The license permitted the theatre company to perform plays in Norwich from 1 November to the end of May every year and for three weeks during the summer including the week in which the Assizes were held. This was a big week in the city's social calendar and attracted visitors from all over the county. As a result of the license, the building - first known as the New Theatre near Chapel Field and then the Grand Concert Hall - adopted the title by which it is still known today, the Theatre Royal. The Norwich Company of Comedians began advertising itself on the playbills as His Majesty's Servants.

The license relieved the company of the need to seek local approval to operate but it did not give it carte blanche. The Lord Chamberlain could send instructions at any time that the theatre would be obliged to follow. This happened two months into the license in May 1768 when the theatre had to be closed for several days because of the death and funeral of HRH Princess Louisa Anne. It happened again in 1772 when the theatre had to be closed for a week because of the death of HRH the Princess Dowager of Wales.

With royal license in hand, Thomas Ivory (until then the sole proprietor) thought the time was right to sell off most of his interest in the theatre and to assume a less-active role in its management. He valued the theatre and its effects at £6000 (about £617,000 adjusted for inflation to 2007). He divided the assets into 30 shares, kept two for himself and offered the remainder for sale. They were taken up by a group of mainly merchants and lawyers (as was the case with those who first invested in the building of the theatre) and not by the names most associated with Norwich's literary and intellectual scene.[29]

On 29 September 1768, Thomas Ivory turned over to Sir William Wiseman, Charles Weston and John Gay (representatives of the new share owners) the Norwich and Colchester theatres and three-quarters of all the costumes and 'standing and movable scenes and decorations' in both theatres. (Under an earlier agreement, the other quarter of the wardrobe and scenery had been passed to the two company members who acted as 'overseers, directors and managers of the wardrobe' - William Henry and Hester Crouse.) The 29 proprietors set up a committee of seven of their members, including Thomas Ivory, to oversee the business of the Norwich theatre and of the circuit. The membership of this executive committee was reviewed each year at a general meeting for all proprietors. The minutes of the meetings both of the committee and the proprietors provides an intriguing insight into the financing and staffing of the theatre in its early days. They detail the amounts paid to the actors and outlays on heating, lighting, maintenance, insurance and extensions and additions. They also detail the legal issues involved in the theatre's management, notably surrounding the various leases. As to wages in 1768, actors earned from £1 1s. 0d. to £1 11s. 6d per week (about £108-£162 in 2007 terms) while musicians earned somewhat less. The leading actors supplemented their incomes by the proceeds of benefit nights organised towards the end of the season.

The Theatre Royal building

The original 1758 building demanded a great deal of maintenance. Heated by coal fires, the chimneys - particularly those in the dressing rooms - needed frequent cleaning. The effects of the smoke from the fireplaces throughout the theatre were compounded by smoke from the oil lamps and, on the special occasions when they were used, by candles. (Gas lighting was only introduced in 1836, some 16 years after gas was available in Norwich; electric lighting came in 1884.) The smoke made frequent redecoration necessary while dampness also caused problems. As the theatre was not in use for the first months of winter it was without heat during this time and dampness set in with deleterious effects on the theatre's fabric. Around the time of the opening of the new season in December 1768, the management advertised that 'Particular care hath been taken to air the house for several weeks past.' Announcements that the house was being kept warm often appear during periods of cold weather. Maintenance costs were also increased by leaks in the roof and by the damage caused by unruly audiences particularly in the gallery. Georgian audiences made a lot of noise by stamping on the floor with their feet or by banging sticks or umbrellas. They often kicked the panels of the boxes as well. In Georgian times, when applause was characterised as being enough 'to bring the house down' the phrase was not entirely figurative. In most off-seasons, the management had to undertake some refurbishment and, on some occasions, make major structural alterations.

In 1799, William Wilkins, a distinguished local builder and architect, applied to take over the lease of the theatre and proposed a major renovation of the building not only to address pressing maintenance issues - particularly on the roof and on the stage -

but also what would now seem horrendous safety concerns. In his analysis, he noted the problems with most parts of the theatre:[30]

The gallery

> one of its approaches being stopped and the remaining outlet very narrow, makes it very long in emptying on full Nights - and there is in consequence a dread which deters many people from entering the House - should there be an alarm only of Fire, this Outlet would be choaked in a few minutes and the destruction of numbers would be the consequence.

The boxes

There were similar problems of egress from the boxes, but Wilkins seemed more concerned about the dresses and sensitivities of the gentle ladies seated in them than of their safety:

> The Entrances and Avenues [to the boxes] are so ill contrived that only one person can approach the Lobby, a Lady must be separated from the Arm of her protector both on entering, leaving the Lobby - The Audience from the Boxes, Green Boxes and pit are here huddled together and on leaving the House they must pass singly to the Entrance where they are obliged to run the Gauntlet thro' Coachmen, Footmen and Porters and if a carriage is not in readiness at the Door it is almost impossible to return 'till the house is nearly emptied, to avoid this bustle and extreme inconvenience, is it not uncommon to see a great part of the Boxes deserted before the end of the Farce; it is really otherways impossible that Ladies can reach their carriages without danger of spoiling their Dresses, and being squeezed perhaps between Doorkeepers, Porters and prostitutes, who are forcing their way without regard to Beauty or Dress.

The orchestra pit

Over the years, the space in front of the stage for the orchestra had been cut back to make room for extra audience seats in the pit. To get enough bowing room, the violinists had to stand up, thereby impeding the sight lines of the audience. Views of the stage were in any case not good for much of the audience because the seating was crowded together and not well raked:

> a number of other inconveniences might also be mention'd, such as the small rise of the Seats in the Boxes and pit, the want of room for the Knees, in sitting &c &c

The lighting

The lighting was also inadequate and the theatre was gloomy:

> The Audience part of the Theatre is become nearly a scene of darkness and more so in the last 8 or 9 years

The stage

Wilkins seemed at a loss to know where to start with the stage:

> With respect to the Stage ... I confess myself by no means prepared to suggest the whole of the improvements necessary to be done there although I am aware of many that must indispensably be made - The machinery to the dropping Scenes, I am informed, are dangerous.

The scenery

According to Wilkins there was 'not a Scene that is worth little more than the Canvas'.

Wilkins was offered the lease and undertook the promised renovations. In 1801, he reported[31] that 'except the walls scarcely any part of the old building remains'. The interior of the theatre was now shaped like an oval with two levels of boxes going right round the theatre with 'four private boxes richly decorated with trellis in gold. … placed upon the stage'. Wilkins also noted that:

> In the accommodation of this part of the house every convenience has been judiciously provided. The entrances are greatly and most conveniently enlarged, and a bar, where refreshments are sold, is added … In the decorative department no expence has been spared; the boxes of the second and upper tiers are lined with painted canvas, some of them provided with proper ventilators, and at the division of each is a gilt pilaster … The pannels are painted with arabesques, the interior devices of which are the emblems of the different dramatic employments.

In enlarging the exit-route corridors, he provided for a greater separation between the different classes of playgoers:

> The avenues of the different parts of the house are separate, by which all disorder in quitting the Theatre is prevented. In short, convenience and beauty are united, and NOVELTY is not a more prevailing feature than TASTE.

The bar was explicitly for the people in the boxes and sold 'tea, coffee, fruit and other refreshments'. (These, of course, were the days before chocolate in solid form had been invented and well before refrigeration and ice cream.)

Wilkins had attempted to make the place brighter by installing 'Patent chandeliers, fashioned after the eastern manner' but there had been a trade-off between brightness and convenience:

> It is however to be regretted, that the Chandeliers will not continue to burn steadily during the hours of the performance without the assistance of the lamplighter; a circumstance which threatens on a full night to involve the audience in darkness.

He had also placed tin shades round the ends of the footlights to avoid the glare that had annoyed people in the side boxes.

Few improvements had been made for those sitting in the cheapest seats in the gallery. They had to be content with the promise that improvements would be made in due course. However, it was difficult to conceive how the main problem - the lowness of the ceiling - would be dealt with.

Problems with the stage, notably the machinery for moving wings and scenery, were remedied. A screen of green baize was erected at the back of the first wing to hide 'the actors from the view of the boxes, till they make their entrance on the boards'. Over the stage, Wilkins hung a coat of arms richly emblazoned in yellow and gold, with the motto: *Conabimur* (we will endeavour). This, he said, was to be 'the device of the company'.

Improvements were also made to the exterior of the building. A colonnade was erected at the front of the building and extensions were pushed out at the sides to widen the exit passageways. The new theatre was well received and local people were proud that Norwich now had one of the handsomest theatres in the provinces.

The renovated Theatre Royal in 1805

Other alterations to the theatre were made over the next two decades, particularly in 1805 - when the stage was widened - and in 1813 and 1814. However, there were limits to what could be done to an old and deteriorating building and round the time of Wilkins' death in 1819, there was no hiding the dilapidation. Increasingly, people began calling for the construction of an entirely new theatre building. And this is exactly what happened in 1825, an event that will be explored in the next chapter.

The plays and the players

Throughout the period, the programming and scheduling of the theatre year remained little changed. Performances in Norwich took place on Monday, Wednesday, Thursday and Saturday evenings generally from round the end of December to the middle of May. (Nightly performances were not introduced until 1842.) The programme would begin at 6.30 o'clock with the main play. This would be followed by musical or dance performances and, on occasion, by a short play or interlude. Finally, there would be a lighter play; most often a farce in the 1760s and, increasingly, a melodrama round the turn of the century. At 8 o'clock, whether the opening play was over or not, half-price tickets were put on sale. This brought in a generally poorer and rowdier element into the gallery and the pit, ready to laugh and heckle at the farce or hiss and cheer at the melodrama. The night's programme proceeded without any intervals and audience members would feel no compunction in walking round and stretching their legs or buying an orange from one of the vendors during the performance. (In 1768, two fruiterers were granted a concession for the season provided that not more than four persons at a time 'attended the house' and that they paid the theatre treasurer 18 pence every night of trading.) Scenery changes took place in full view of the audience because it was not possible to make short blackouts. Members of the audience closest to the stage would have heard audible signals from backstage: whistles for sceneshifters and bells for the orchestra.

The management recognised that the financial viability of the theatre depended on the entrance fees of the mass audience on the backless benches of the pit and the gallery. However, both management and actors would have much preferred a larger presence of the gentry and the better-educated classes. To persuade such people to become regular attenders was one of the managers' constant preoccupations. In 1783, an 'admirer of the Drama and a constant attendant on the Theatre' (perhaps a pseudonym for the theatre manager or owner?) wrote to the *Norfolk Chronicle* recommending to the 'principal inhabitants' of Norwich that they copy the practice of their class in 'most other towns in the kingdom … not to give or receive public visits on a play-night'. 'How', the anonymous correspondent continued, 'can the proprietors afford to give new scenery, dresses, etc, unless the receipts of the house are adequate; or, can a performer play with so much spirit to empty benches?'[32]

The quality of the scenery could increase the number of people buying seats. This was particularly the case for the special scenic effects in melodramas. A good example of this was Robert Dixon's ravine and rocky gorge - complete with drawbridge and explosions - designed for the 1814 melodrama *The Miller and His Men*. Mr Thorne, who took over after the death of Dixon, attracted patrons to see his grand-moving panorama that started with a view of ships lying in the basin of the planned port of Norwich leading through Thorpe and on to the grand junction lock at Lowestoft. In 1823, audience numbers were swelled by those wanting to see the exact representation of a treadmill being turned by a group of unfortunate prisoners.

The playbill advertising Mr Dixon's scenery in the Miller and His Men

Audiences had little chance of booking ahead to see a particular play because the programmes were rarely decided more than a few days in advance. In fact, on a Monday morning, actors would often not know which plays they would be performing on Wednesday or Thursday evenings. Sometimes the programme for the next night would be announced from the stage. This was a source of irritation for the public and, in 1778, the manager, Richard Griffith, tried to defend himself:

> Mr Griffith would be happy to have it in his power to comply with the desire of several ladies and gentlemen … by advertising the particular plays proposed to be performed in each ensuing week; but the frequent indispositions which the performers are liable to, particularly at this severe season of the year, and the limited number of actors to which, at present, it seems necessary to confine the company, put it out of his power to advertise a week's plays together, with any certainty of their being represented at the time proposed.[33]

The choice of plays for each performance would generally be made by the manager based on which pieces his company had in their repertoire and which ones the local playgoers were most likely to pay to see. Some of the programmes, though, were 'bespeaks'. These were evenings where wealthy patrons, such as the lord mayor or local societies such as masonic orders or the officers of a regiment, would select a play (or plays) from the repertoire and then buy up a substantial number of tickets to sell on or to give away. For their 'bespeaks', the masons would sometimes meet at their chapter house and march in full regalia to the theatre. These were obviously popular with the theatre management not only because of the guaranteed ticket sales but also because the higher the social status of the sponsor of the 'bespeak', the more 'quality' patrons were likely to attend.

Towards the end of the season, several programmes would be 'benefit nights' for specified actors or others associated with the theatre's operations. The proceeds from the ticket sales (with the exception of an agreed sum paid to the theatre) would go directly to the beneficiary. Actors were very careful in putting together an attractive programme for their benefit nights because the proceeds provided an essential part of their annual earnings. Sometimes they would write material of their own for the performance. In 1799, the proceeds from a benefit night varied from £46 to £100 (or from nearly £3000 to £6000 at 2007 prices).

John Bernard, who was part of the Norwich Company of Comedians in the 1770s, wrote up some fascinating memories of the off-stage life of the actors.[34] In 1774, while he was pursuing the hard life of a strolling player, he found himself one night in the small market town of Dedham, just south of Ipswich in what is now known as Constable Country. Coincidentally, two Norwich aldermen - a Mr Day and John Gay, the latter a part-proprietor of Norwich Theatre Royal - were in the audience. They were impressed by his performance and invited him back to take supper with them at their inn. Three days later, Bernard received a letter from Mr Griffith inviting him to join the company to 'play the fops and light comedy' at a salary of thirty shillings a week. Bernard was elated, not only because of the enormous increase in his salary but also because of the prestige of working in a theatre that 'ranked next to Bath out of the metropolis'. His fellow strollers were acutely jealous. One sneered that 'it was a pity that some people did not know when they were well off' and another called Gay and Day 'worstead-headed weavers without any judgment'.

Bernard left post-haste for Norwich and was thrilled by the more professional world that he found. He described his new boss, Griffith - who had come to Norwich from the theatre in Dublin about ten years earlier - as 'a perfect beau of the old school, a Sir Philip Modelove in real life', whose character contrasted with some of the more workaday members of the company. Bernard recalls how, one morning, *Much Ado about Nothing* had been 'called'. Griffith began the rehearsal but was called away to meet with the proprietors in the committee room. He left his annotated copy of the play - 'very elegantly bound and embellished and enriched with marginal notes from his own pen'- behind on a table. One of the actors, Robert Bowles, flicked through the book and saw that Griffith had noted that Benedick (Griffith's part) 'should look at least five and thirty - should be manly and even elegant'. Seeing no note about Borachio (the part he was to play), he grabbed a pen and scribbled 'in a scraggy hand': 'Borachio should be a lean long-backed fellow, with sandy hair and red hands, fond of nothing but fishing.' The background to this is that Bowles was known to be a keen fisherman and never wore gloves 'which rendered his hands on a cold day like two pieces of raw beef'. Griffith often commented to Bowles about his vulgar appearance. As might be imagined from this and the two stories recounted later, Bowles was a better comedian than a serious actor. Of his performances in King's Lynn in 1802, one reviewer wrote:

> Mr Bowles ... whenever he appears in comedy is not altogether destitute of merit; but in tragedy - laud him ye Gods!!!
>
> But what does BOWLES? - why lifts both hands and then
> Drops down his right, and - lifts it up again!
> Meanwhile a sort of quack compounding grace
> Pervades his whole circumference of face[35]

Despite his eccentricities, Griffith was a great teacher and motivator. Under his tutelage, Bernard noted that 'such was my enthusiasm for acting then, that it constituted not only my means of subsistence but my sole source of enjoyment'. Moreover, 'the various bad habits and ideas I had contracted in my eight months itinerancy speedily disappeared'. Bernard fitted in well with the company and observed that the proceeds from his benefit performances proved his 'rising favour with the public'. He seems to have got to know this public well. He recalled how Norwich families used to send their servants to the box office in the morning to inquire what was playing that same evening and how these servants would return home and report that the main play was *The Boar Strangled (The Beaux Stratagem)* or *The Virgin Mary (Virgin Unmasked)*.

Bernard could hardly believe his good luck - 'fame and fortune were thus flowing in upon me who seven months before had struggled for shillings and "strutted and fretted" on the flooring of barns'. The professional company still took to the road, however, and could find itself in competition with strolling players and entertainers, particularly in some towns of the circuit outside of Norwich. He remembered that the company did not do well at Bury because of the competition from Mrs Baker's booth 'where the public bill of fare put forth a greater variety and more piquant dishes than ours'. Griffith was disgusted at the public's taste:

No wonder that thefts and drunkenness and distress so abound when people go to booths instead of theatres and prefer seeing a mountebank stand on his head, to an able trage-dian in the character of Hamlet.[36]

Bernard spent ten months with the company and left Norwich with about £80 in his pocket 'a sum that at one time I did not think was possessable by an entire company'. He went on to a successful career as an actor and later manager in London and in North America.

Mr Chalmers of the Norwich Company of Comedians in the role of Midas c. 1774

The Theatre Royal management had many successes in finding and training actors for greater things. It also had its failures. In 1770, Elizabeth Simpson wrote from her home near Bury, seeking to follow in the footsteps of her brother George in getting employment with the Norwich Company of Comedians. Griffith sent her a classic 'don't-call-me-I'll-call-you' response:

> Madam,
> I was just favoured with yours - the purpose of which, depend upon it, shall be an entire secret. From some treaties which I have now depending with different performers and some proposals given under my hand, until I have received answers to them, I cannot yet say it is in my power, as much as it is in my inclination to oblige you: if it should be, be assured I shall be happy to do it.

The person he turned down later became Elizabeth Inchbald, who acted successfully in Bristol and other provincial theatres and became one of the leading playwrights of her generation.

Elizabeth Inchbald

Two stories about Richard Griffith and the Norwich Company of Comedians in the 1770s

Griffith bonded well with the acting company and on days off would sometimes organise fishing parties. He paid for the carriages and the company members chipped in for refreshment. Griffith was a litte short-sighted and 'extremely nice in his hands and clothes'. He would get someone to bait his hook (a 'piece of dirty drudgery') and would then stand for hours on the brink of the stream, taking snuff and holding his rod in his white-gloved hand in 'a variety of elegant attitudes'. One day all but Griffith had caught something. The practical joker of the company, Robert Bowles, told him to take some refreshment while he held his rod. Griffith agreed and helped himself to cold fowl and punch from the basket. While he was away, Bowles took a large Yarmouth herring from his pocket, hooked it on Griffith's line and threw it back. Later another member of the company asked Griffith how he was doing. Griffith, whose repetitive style of speech was similar to Garrick's, replied:

> Sport, sport - why, why, not so bad - plenty of fish, plenty of fish - good bait you see, good bait - Bobby minds that - shady spot - deep hole there - all quiet, all quiet, had a hundred offers from the small fry, but wouldn't take 'em - plenty of bites but caught nothing.

Someone then shouted that his float had been pulled under and Griffith reeled it in excitely calling on Bowles to take the fish for him. Bowles looked at the herring and exclaimed that he had never seen a finer mullet. Griffith was at first unsure that it was a mullet but was convinced by the company. He took it home for supper and when, the following morning, he was asked how he had liked the mullet replied he had 'never partaken of a finer'.

One year before this, Griffith and Bowles and two local gentlemen went out shooting. Seeing that Griffith was not catching anything, Bowles tricked him by assuring him that he had hit one and that it had fallen behind the barn. They rushed to the spot and found an 'old weather-beaten, broken backed, bandy-legged duck, limping by'. Bowles persuaded Griffith that was the one he winged. Griffith chased after it and the noise brought out the farmer, who shouted at them that that particular duck could not have been shot. It had been 'a patriarch in his puddles these six years and hadn't wing enough to fly over a turnip'. Bowles then surreptitiously bribed the farmer to change his story and Griffith went home with the duck in his bag. The farmer and his workers 'opened their capacious jaws and lowed out their laughter like so many oxen'.

From John Bernard Retrospections of the Stage *130-132*

Major changes to the management of the theatre were agreed in the 1780s. Until then, the theatre proprietors had taken a fairly hands-on approach to the day-to-day running of it working with an appointed manager. However, things were not going well and audience numbers and receipts were in decline. A prolonged spell of bad weather at the beginning of the 1784 season made matters worse and pushed income well below expenses. About this time Lady Jerningham wrote from France to her daughter:

> We remained all Monday at Lille. Lady Charlotte Radcliffe came and dined with us and I went to the play with her. A tolerable theatre, but as empty of company as the Norwich playhouse is of a common night.[37]

The proprietors then decided to lease out the theatre for an annual sum and thus assure themselves of income from their investment without having to carry out tasks for which they were not well qualified. The first lessee, Giles Barrett, who agreed to pay £180 per annum for the lease, brought new life to the theatre. One of his first plans was to make annual tickets available. The *Norfolk Chronicle* reported:

> Ladies and Gentlemen desirous of holding Annual Tickets of Admission from the first of January 1785 to the commencement of the Benefits are most respectfully informed that subscription will be received at the Barrett's No. 50 Bethel Street till the 31st inst - tickets delivered at 2 guineas each, entitles the subscriber to free Admittance on every play-night to any part of the Theatre before the curtain; at 3 guineas the ticket of Admission is transferable to any one of the subscriber's family, named at the time of subscribing.[38]

The beginning of Barrett's first season went extremely well according to the local press:

Lady Jerningham

> 1 Jan 1785: Audience far more numerous than we ever recollect at a 1st night - high satisfaction at improvements made - great taste & elegance … the Norwich Theatre may at this time vie with any in the kingdom for its beauty.

> 18 Jan 1785: Theatre has for some years been on the decline, but is once more likely to become the fashionable resort of the opulent.

> 25 Jan 1785: great company, pit and gallery overflowed … front of house lighted with wax … the gods as usual clamorous for their favourite dance.

Four years later, the lease was taken over by John Brunton, who was to lead the Theatre Royal through one of its golden periods. Brunton, born in Norwich in 1741 the son of a soapmaker, became a grocer and took over a shop in London's theatre district in Drury Lane. He must have been a regular playgoer before he persuaded one of the acting companies to take him on as a member. He played Hamlet at Covent Garden in 1774 and the following year returned home to play the same role under the direction of Mr Griffith with the Norwich Company of Comedians. It was a resounding success and he became the company's leading tragedian for the next five years before moving on to play at Bath and elsewhere. Small and with 'little piercing eyes',[39] he was particularly good in playing Shylock and Richard III. Often referred to as the 'Northern Roscius', he and his wife and three of his daughters built up strong reputations. His daughter, Ann, was reckoned by many to be on a par with Mrs Sarah Siddons while another daughter, Louisa, married the Earl of Craven, an early example of peers marrying actresses. His sons, Richard and John, also appeared on the Norwich stage but did not pursue acting as a career. John became a surgeon practicing in Mattishall (a few miles west of Norwich) and Richard went into the army.

> **Roscius**
> Quintus Roscius, c 126 BC - 62BC, had the reputation of being Rome's greatest comic actor. In the 18th and 19th centuries, therefore, outstanding actors of the British stage were honoured and bestowed with the title Roscius, hence 'the Northern Roscius'.

In 1788, Brunton bought the lease of the Theatre Royal and took over as manager, a post he retained until 1800. Securing Brunton's services for the Theatre Royal was seen as a great coup. His address to the audience on his first night in charge was greeted with 'tremendous applause such as never heard before'. He arrived on the eve of the French Revolution at a time when Norwich was gaining a name for itself as a home for political radicals questioning the legitimacy of Britain's political institutions. In the years following the French Revolution in 1789, Norwich intellectual life was seen as being divided into two camps: one - known for its Jacobin sympathies and associated with William Enfield, the Minister of the Unitarian Church - met at the Octagon Chapel (another Thomas Ivory building); and the other - known for its more royalist and conservative views and associated with John Brunton - met at the Theatre Royal.[40] During his period in charge, Brunton refused to stage *Elmira* written by Stanley (one of his actors) because of its radical thrust but agreed to mount a production of *Huniades or the Siege of Belgrade,* a play with a clear anti-revolutionary message written by another local performer, Hannah Brand. Brunton was unlikely to have had Jacobin sympathies

Elizabeth Brunton 1799-1860

himself, but even if he had, he would have probably suppressed them so as to keep in well with his traditional patrons.

During his period in charge, Brunton put together a strong group of actors and established close working relations with the professional stage in London. Samuel Taylor Coleridge wrote to Southey of the company's regular circuit visit to Stourbridge Fair near Cambridge:

> It is our Sturbritch Fair Time and the Norwich Company are theatricalising. They are the first provincial Actors in the Kingdom.[41]

He was probably right, but in fairness, it should be acknowledged that he was rather attracted by Brunton's daughter, Elizabeth.

Brunton was considerate of his actors and in 1791 he set up a new 'fund for the relief of those performers belonging to the Theatre who, thro' age or infirmity might be obliged to retire from the stage'. He planned to hold an annual benefit performance where all the proceeds would be used to supplement its capital. Acting continued to be a strenuous profession both physically and mentally. There are many stories of actors performing while ill in the 'show-must-go-on' tradition. However, this was not always appreciated by audiences and in February 1783 a correspondent to the local paper wrote about an actor obviously labouring with memory, speech and movement:

> We very much lament the necessity of wishing that Mr Banister would, until his health is restored, retire from the stage.

Some years later Mr Bellamy became so ill at the end of a performance:

> as to require immediate surgical aid; he was effectively relieved by opening a vein; and is now, we hope, likely to do well.

Mr Bellamy (whose vein had to be opened) as Dr Pangloss

Touring at the end of the long Norwich season, with all the travel and staying in places that provided few home comforts, could be particularly wearing and - this being the age of the highwayman - also dangerous. One Sunday evening in November 1789:

> Mr C. Powell of the Norwich Company of Comedians was returning from Ipswich when he was stopped by two footpads … robbed and finger nearly bit through.

The company actors had to be able to switch from one play to another with one rehearsal - that is if there was time for one. John Bernard confirmed that an essential skill of actors during his time at Norwich was the ability to commit several roles to memory at once. It was not unusual for an actor on one night to play King Richard, sing two comic songs, dance a hornpipe and then finish the night as Harlequin. To save the effort of learning new lines, many clung on tenaciously to one part in the plays in the repertoire and were unwilling to cede it to another member of the company. When new plays were being prepared, the actors were only given their own lines, so as to avoid unauthorised full copies being sold or passed on. (This was true in Shakespeare's day, too, and helps to explain how imperfect transcribing led to so many different versions of his plays.) The short time for memorisation and rehearsal and the shortage of well-prepared understudies meant frequent flawed performances where a part would be read, important speeches skipped over, entrances late or from the wrong side of the stage and scenes or characters simply left out.

In fact, rehearsals were generally only for blocking and repetition of lines with there being a general understanding that it would be 'alright on the night'. In fact, it was frequently not 'alright on the night' and the prompter was often called into action. One critic, Richard Bacon, left some interesting insights into the Theatre Royal experience in 1799; he spoke of actors forgetting lines and of resort to shabby and recycled costumes and scenery. Speaking of the acting ensemble, he wrote of them being 'contemptibly deficient':

> When four or five happened to be upon the stage at a time, conscious of individual imbecility, they huddled together like sheep for mutual defence and assistance.

Of Mr Seymour, one of the actors, Bacon wrote:

> Lo, Seymour comes unwilling to the scene
> Too negligent to get the words by rote
> Too absent to remember them if got
> He twitches, stammers, stamps and thinks in vain
> Lifts his right arm, then lets it fall again
> Thrusts out his neck, and in confusion waits
> The fatal line for which he hesitates
> The fatal line, the friendly prompter gives,
> Again he stops, again his friend relieves. [42]

Superstitions

There were several superstitions in Georgian rehearsals including the practice of never saying out loud the 'bank' (the closing lines of the play). This superstition persists in pantomime through to this day and at the Theatre Royal the final lines of the show are never uttered before the first performance.

Sophia Goddard was another actor who sometimes forgot her lines. Bacon noted that this was because she was asked to take on too many parts and it would not have happened if she had had more time to concentrate; a pity because her 'genius promises greatness'. Interestingly, when Sophia died two years later (aged only 25) her death was attributed to the over-exertions in her career. The newspaper obituary stated:

> The energies of her mind impelled her to efforts too mighty for her corporeal powers, and she had fallen an early victim to professional exertions. [43]

Her tomb can still be seen in the churchyard outside the 'actors church' of St Peter Mancroft.

Bacon accuses another member of the company of allowing her vanity to spoil the quality of her performance:

> Mrs Taylor possesses a most sweet, powerful, and extensive voice, but unfortunately she also has the most beautiful set of teeth. To display these, she extends her mouth so unmercifully, that some parts of her intonation are scarcely human; in singing her articulation is totally destroyed, and in speaking frequently impeded.

Another member of the company, he claimed, acted with 'one fixed stare of low grimace'.

Bacon criticised Brunton for cutting costs on scenery and costumes. This was the year that Wilkins had reported on the dilapidated state of the theatre and its scenery referring particularly to a performance of *Bluebeard*:

> The gorgeous procession in Bluebeard shall remain for ages unequalled in elegance of design, unrivalled in splendour of execution! Ten dirty and tattered accoutrements for the slaves, four flags, one brass-hilted sword, one gilded wheelbarrow … and one newly painted palanquin made up the grand display of dresses and decorations exhibited at this sumptuous and superb solemnity. Most magnificent procession! Most magnificent manager!

The company seems to have enjoyed a good esprit de corps and, in 1798, when there were fears of a possible French invasion, the local newspaper reported:

> We understand that the performers in our theatre have come to the resolution of forming themselves into a volunteer corps for the defence of the country; and that their services are to extend to any part of the Eastern district, in case of actual invasion.[44]

From time to time, eminent actors and actresses from the London stage joined the Norwich Company of Comedians and their visits often led to great excitement in the county and a rush for tickets. This was certainly the case for Mrs Sarah Siddons' visit in 1788.

At the time of her visit, Norwich was better developed than it had been on the theatre's opening night 30 years before. But a walk to the theatre in the evening would still have been difficult and not without danger. A trade directory published just a few years before noted how the roads were horribly paved and often without names or signposts. Many of them were so narrow that pedestrians had

> to press against walls or burst into shops to avoid getting run down. In wet weather they get splashed or have to walk into deep puddles.

The writers found the air to be stale and recommended taking down the gates and levelling the medieval city wall to improve its circulation. While there were some good inns and reasonable boarding-houses,

> there is great want of Hotel and Tavern to accommodate genteel families, parties, or persons of rank.[45]

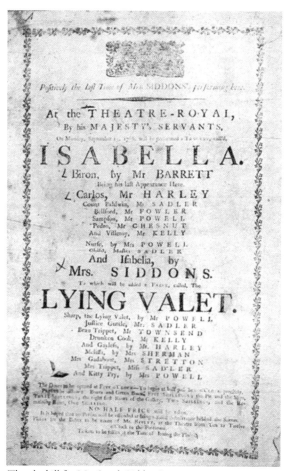

The playbill for Mrs Sarah Siddons' 1788 visit

According to the directory, during the week the city had an empty and melancholy air and it only came alive on Sundays and public holidays when the weavers were able to leave their looms.

Mrs Siddons (née Sarah Kemble) built up a strong and enviable reputation in provincial theatre companies in York and Bath and then went on to conquer Drury Lane in 1782, where she made an instant sensation playing the lead role in *Isabell or The Fatal Marriage*. For the next 20 years she was the undisputed leading actress in the country and when she agreed to play Norwich in 1788 she was at the height of her fame. Her engagement was certainly the biggest event in the theatre's history and triggered excitement round the county. A month before her arrival, Norwich inns and lodging-houses were already getting booked up by people who intended 'partaking of this dramatic treat'.[46] The Theatre Royal raised ticket prices by more than 40 per cent for the occasion, bringing the cost of a seat in the boxes to five shillings. There were some spare seats for her first performance but on the second and third nights the theatre was overflowing. Audiences were not disappointed and they soon fell under the spell of her 'strong and flexible features' and, in particular, of her 'large and penetrating eyes'. The intensity of her acting was, for many, overwhelming. In Norwich, this was particularly the case when she played two of her signature roles: the eponymous heroine in *The Tragedy of Jane Shore* and Lady Randolph in Home's *Douglas*. In *The Tragedy of Jane Shore*, Mrs Siddons played the part of the beautiful Jane whose life spiralled down from one of luxury and jollity as King Edward IV's mistress to one of penury and humiliation begging as a 'lean, withered and dried up'[47] old woman on the streets of London. In *Douglas*, she played Lady Randolph who is unaware that her young son, whom she lost and supposed dead, had been found and brought up by a shepherd. The boy reappears, saves the life of his stepfather, Lord Randolph, and is reunited with great emotion with his mother. But Lord Randolph's heir fears that his inheritance is threatened and kills his newfound stepbrother. Lady Randolph is overwhelmed with grief and throws herself from a cliff. The part has many heart-rending speeches that Mrs Siddons played with great dramatic gestures, choked voice and the necessary tears:

> The love of thee, before thou saw'st the light
> Sustain'd my life when thy brave father fell,
> If thou shalt fall, I have not love not hope
> In this waste world! My son, remember me!

Reports from London state that when Mrs Siddons played such roles in the capital she was often greeted by shrieking and sobbing in the audience. She had much the same reaction in Norwich. As the *Norwich Mercury* reported:

> The faintings of some of the female part of the audience with the many fair faces suffused with tears, added to the glistening eyes of the other sex, have borne ample testimony of her unequalled powers.[48]

Mrs Siddons' nine-day season in Norwich boosted both the theatre and the local economy. Proceeds totalled £852 of which Mrs Siddons took away £423 (£79,000 and £39,000 respectively in 2007 prices).

Mrs Siddons in rehearsal

Mrs Siddons' younger brother, Charles Kemble, was a guest star performer at the Theatre Royal in 1817 but made only a modest impact, as did Charles Matthews, another well-known London actor, who had visited some weeks earlier.

Charles Kemble as Othello

Playbill announcing Charles Kemble's 1835 visit

40

Henry Wallack of the Norwich Company as Timour the Tartar c. 1815

..and as Alcibrades

In the following year, however, the management attracted to Norwich the then acknowledged greatest male actor of his period and, to many, of all time, Edmund Kean. Ten years earlier, Mrs Siddons had dismissed Kean as a horrid, little man, who was unlikely to make a great actor. But after a number of ups and downs, Kean became a sensation after a season of Shakespearian roles at Drury Lane in 1814. His ability to act a wide range of tragic emotions mesmerised audiences. When he came to Norwich in 1817, he played two of his most famous Shakespearian roles, the hunchbacked Richard III and the moor Othello. In the latter play, it was reported that:

> The agony of mind which he betrayed on discovering the villainy of Iago, and the innocence of his murdered wife and the solemn and affecting tone in which he delivered his concluding speech before he stabs himself, drew tears from many.

The way in which Kean used his whole body to portray a role emerges from the report that his

> dying attitude after he had smote himself might have served as a copy for the painter or as a model for the statuary.[49]

Richard Jones of the Norwich Company as Sir Francis Faddle

The Norwich audience reacted particularly favourably to Kean's performance in Massinger's *A New Way to Pay Old Debts*. In this play, Kean was able to showcase his histrionic skills as Sir Giles Overreach, a money-grabbing extortionist.

Edmund Kean as Sir Giles Overreach

During the final scene the peals of applause continued so long that nothing more could be heard of the play - the performers retired - and the curtain fell.

Kean returned to act in Norwich in 1819 and 1830. During his 1819 visit (at the age of 32) he played Richard III when 'he indulged in the unhappy propensity which shortened his life'. He was arrested in the market place in character of Richard III brandishing two brass candlesticks and crying: 'My kingdom for a horse.' He was bundled into the clink under the Guildhall and appeared the next morning in court with two black eyes to face a lecture from the mayor of Norwich. Despite advice to the contrary, the bishop of Norwich, Bishop Bathurst, maintained his invitation to Kean to call on him that afternoon to give him a private performance of some of his favourite scenes. This kept him sober for the rest of his Norwich engagement.[50]

Edmund Kean as Hamlet

The excitement created by the appearances of both Mrs Siddons and Edmund Kean were eclipsed by the frenzy seen in 1818 when the tragedienne, Eliza O'Neill, came to the city. Born in Ireland, she started her career there before coming to London. And, like Kean, it was in 1814 that she moved into superstar celebrity status on the London stage. When it was announced that she would be appearing in Norwich for six nights in September, the demand for tickets was unprecedented. The box office was besieged every morning and the management had to quell rumours by assuring the public that no seats would be disposed of before the box office opened. When the doors were flung open in the evening, people struggled to get their seats on a 'first-come-first-served' basis. The *Norfolk Chronicle* reported that:

> No law prevailed but that of the strongest … the spirit of politeness and gallantry maintained only a very feeble influence over the conduct of the assembled multitude - nothing was heard but shrieks, reproaches and lamentations- nothing to be seen but bonnets cramped up, hats squeezed flat, torn gown and coat flaps, and a motley crowd in the highest state of exasperation, fermentation and perspiration.[51]

Not every one from the higher social ranks could find a seat in the boxes and many had to rub shoulders with the lesser orders in other parts of the theatre or, as the paper reported, 'families of the highest respectability were in inconvenient situations'. It seems that there was some overbooking because some people crowded into the orchestra space.

O'Neill lived up to her great reputation and gripped audiences with her performance of Juliet in *Romeo and Juliet*. It is easy to imagine the tears flowing as she approached her final moments over Romeo's dead body:

> I will kiss thy lips;
> Haply some poison yet doth hang on them,
> To make die with a restorative.

Her most powerful emotional impact, though, was as Belvidera in *Venice Preserved*. In the final act of the play she has to react to the death of her husband caused by the pursuit of a moral course of action that she had urged him to take. The final act gave her several breast-beating speeches:

> Curs'd be my days, and doubly curs'd my nights,
> Which I must now mourn out in widow'd tears;
> Blasted be every herb and fruit and tree;
> Curs'd be the rain that falls upon the earth,
> And may the general curse reach man and beast;
> Oh, give me daggers, fire or water!

And then her heart finally breaks and she collapses on the stage:

> My love! My dear! My blessing!
> Help me, help me!
> They've hold on me, and drag me to the bottom.
> Nay - now they pull so hard – farewell

The correspondent of the *Norfolk Chronicle* claimed to have been left speechless by her performances - a rather amusing figure of speech given the impossibly florid prose in which the claim was made:

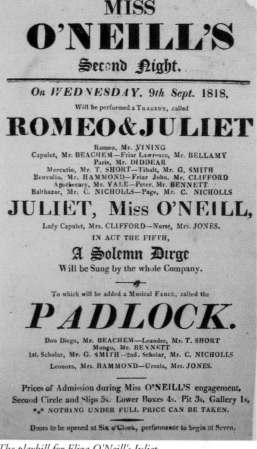

The playbill for Eliza O'Neill's Juliet

Eliza O'Neill as Belvidera (courtesy of Wolverhampton Art Gallery + Museums)

…we are at a loss for words to express what we think of endowments so various, so rare, so excellent as hers, or of that felicitous combination of knowledge and skill, by which she develops all the passions with such delightful influence, such affecting truth, such imposing and irresistible force, nor would we, even though we ran the risk of being deficient in the faculty of discriminative observation, alloy the pleasures of memory, arising to us out of the enjoyment of so rich a treat, by studiously seeking for reasons to justify our making the smallest abatement in the measure either of our admiration or our praise.[52]

Ticket receipts averaged £200 at each performance. O'Neill received £700 (nearly £38,000 at 2007 prices) somewhat less than Mrs Siddons had taken home in 2007 terms but it was for fewer performances. Norwich audiences were among the last to see her perform because, less than a year later, aged only 28, she left the London stage and married an Irish Member of Parliament, William Becher. She became Lady Becher after her husband's knighthood and died more than 50 years later in 1872.

One other famous actor who came to the Theatre Royal in 1818 stayed with the company for a period. His name was Junius Brutus Booth. Although a well-known actor in his day, he is remembered now mainly as the father of John Wilkes Booth, the assassin of Abraham Lincoln.

Junius Brutus Booth of the Norwich Company

While Norwich audiences were occasionally regaled by performances by the foremost actors in the land, they also had to sit through performances given by untrained amateurs who had paid the management to let them act. The management connived at this because of the income it generated by any fee and by the extra tickets that would be purchased by the debutant's colleagues, friends and family. Sometimes the performances were promising and held the audience but more frequently they were dire and triggered jeers and laughter from the audience. The newspaper reviews varied from politely dismissive -

When he has conquered that awkward diffidence, so natural to persons, who have not acquired stage address, he may afford us a happier presage of his rising above mediocrity.[53]

- to outright scorn

[Mr Payne of Norwich] 'succeeded only in exciting the risibility of the other performers and loud peals of laughter from the audience, mixed with some marks of disapprobation.'[54]

And a few years later about an amateur Hamlet:

if the debutant had had one judicious friend, he would not have exposed himself to the ridicule which his performance met from a numerous audience.[55]

The 1819 performance by Mr Payne prompted the *Norwich Mercury* to write a verse:

Let Mortal man his grief and care give o'er,
Nor crave the aid of potion or of pill;
For Payne now makes our sides with laughter sore,
And, tho' he threatens, yet - neglects to kill.

Some actors from the Norwich Company of Comedians round the turn of the 19th century

Mrs Faucit as Cleopatra

Above: Mr Bennett as Ziekde Homespun
Left: Mr Vining as Octavian

The audiences

Accounts of Mrs Siddons' 1788 appearance at the Theatre Royal give us a clear picture of how the audience looked.

> The oil lamps and candles shone upon a magnificent array of feathers and flowers...and wigs and ruffles. Country families who had braved disagreeable journeys over wretched roads...jostled with opulent citizens and their dames; and military officers and city beaux quizzed Norwich beauties and criticised the wondrous toilets that met their gaze on every side.[56]

Long feathers were in fashion at this time and in many public places rooms were set aside for women to put their feathered headpieces on as they were too tall to be worn in a covered carriage. The fashion obviously impeded good sight lines. One correspondent, who signed himself as 'a man of diminutive size', appealed to the Theatre Royal manager to recommend

> on this extraordinary occasion that ladies will for once make a small sacrifice by wearing simpler head-dresses at the theatre during Mrs Siddons's performance, for the dignity of her face and person will make her a great object to be seen as well as heard.[57]

It seems that this plea might have been successful as the newspaper later reported

> The gentleman are agreeably flattered .. with the condescension of the ladies in having formed a resolution to dress without caps or hats, during the performance in September, as they shall then have an opportunity of being gratified with a view of their faces, as well as those of the performers, an advantage they very seldom obtained, during all the last season, when those abominable extinguishers to grace and beauty, the large hats and enormous caps, were so universally in fashion.[58]

Georgian audiences were vastly different from their contemporary counterparts, particularly in terms of their emotional sensitivity and propensity to tears and in their unruliness and lack of discipline. Indeed, the silence and emotional reserve of today's audiences would seriously unnerve any returning 18th-century actors. They would also, no doubt, find it difficult to adopt an acting style that did not have to address the issue of acting against the background hubbub caused by people milling about and chatting between themselves. Late into the century, the management continued to implore audience members - mainly from the higher social classes - not to walk behind the stage during performances.

> It is hoped that no gentleman will take offence at being refused admittance behind the scenes. The Committee, having received frequent complaints that great hindrances in working the machinery and other inconveniences have arisen therefrom, have given positive orders to the door keeper to admit no person whatever.[59]

Eight years later, the problem was as bad as ever and the management seems to have struggled to draft a press release with the required deference and diplomacy:

> As repeated Interruptions and Inconveniencies have arisen from admitting Persons behind the Scenes, the Manager Hopes no Offence will be taken from his being under the indispensable Necessity of informing the Public, that to prevent any Dispute or Disturbance in future, No One (not belonging to the Theatre) can on any Account or Pretence (during the Time of the Performance) gain Admittance to the Stage Door.[60]

Georgian audiences can, in many ways, be likened to the football crowd of today. The better-off citizens would be in the boxes akin to the football hospitality suites and, much as today, would be talking business and gossiping and not concentrating their whole attention on the play. In any case, some of them would have arrived late and would not know exactly what the play was about. Fielding spoke of the women who came into theatre boxes:

> to show themselves, spread their fans upon the spikes, make curtsies to their acquaintances, and then talk and laugh as loud as they are able.[61]

The bulk of the audience in the pit, akin to the closer seats to the football pitch, would be engaged in the play but would be quite vocal throughout, applauding any good moves but whistling and jeering at any player who fluffed lines or failed to impress.

A caricature of a provincial audience in 1807

Then there would be the small hardcore of troublemakers mostly in the cheapest seats of the gallery - the ancestors of today's football hooligans - who would be drunk and still drinking and liable to vandalise and cause whatever type of commotion that amused them. Sometimes their behaviour could be dangerous to others. In 1783 a glass bottle was thrown from the gallery on to the stage. The same occurred in 1821 but this time the culprit was arrested and imprisoned:

> On Wednesday night last, some person most wantonly threw a glass bottle from the gallery upon the stage. Mr Smith, the manager, attended by the mayor's officers, immediately went up and with a laudable perseverance discovered the offender, who proved to be a young man of the name of Wheeler (son of the late Mr Wheeler formerly of this theatre). He was lodged in Bridewell, and on Thursday committed by the mayor to the same prison for the space of one month, for the offence.[62]

Visiting soldiers were also often badly behaved in the theatre. Ann Ditchell wrote to a friend in the early 1790s when there were frequent tensions between the military and the local population:

Norwich is like the country dull for those who live in it - even the Theatre is become a scene of terror for the Ladies since the last regiment of soldiers arrived; it is not unusual now for the officers to break their swords with fighting & rioting at the Theatre, while the common soldiers are insulting & disgracing themselves & human nature in the streets: however, I am happy to say some few regulations have been made to prevent such depredations on the public peace in future.[63]

Audiences, the King and the National Anthem

Two pieces of background to the story of the soldiers: first, Norwich had a (not entirely justified) reputation of being a city with Jacobin sympathies and this would not have gone down well with soldiers fighting against the French revolutionary armies; and second, it had become quite customary around this time to sing the national anthem as an expression of concern for the illness of King George III. It was often audiences who called for the cast to sing the song rather than the management and sometimes, to the annoyance of the actors, it could be called for four or five times during the course of an evening. Parson Woodforde was an occasional visitor to the theatre and he recalled a 1794 performance where the national anthem was sung 'with great glee'.

Parson Woodforde who visited the Theatre Royal in 1794

The most serious problem with soldiers occurred in 1800 with officers recently transferred from Ireland to Norwich. They called for the national anthem to be sung after the first play of the evening. When the second play started without the anthem being sung, they considered the management and audience disrespectful, drew their swords and cleared the house, bruising some spectators and damaging clothes. Five of the soldiers were apprehended and at the Quarter Sessions some weeks later the four ensigns and one lieutenant pleaded guilty to causing a riot and were fined £5 each.

Audiences, on occasion, halted the actors in their tracks by shouting out demands. Actors were seen in a different light in the 18th and early 19th centuries; they were perceived to be the servants of the people over whom it was not unnatural for an audience to want to exert some power. In April 1823, after the conclusion of the first play *Adeline or The Victim of Seduction*, loud calls were made for one member of the company, Mr Sloman, to sing a song. The calls were ignored and the second play, *The Duel*, began. Then the audience high up in the gods (the gallery) rose up:

> their high mightinesses the gods thundered out their disapprobation and *The Duel* became immediately dumb show.[64]

The manager only managed to restore enough peace to continue with the programme by explaining that the subject of a benefit night made his own choice of programme and this could not be changed.

Actors in the days before sound amplification and proper lighting had to work hard to keep their audience with them and would structure into their performances speeches or pieces of business designed to trigger applause - the 'clap-traps'. They would pause at the end of these moments to wait for the applause rather like at the end of a song in a contemporary musical. It was, of course, embarrassing if no applause was forthcoming. Actors had to work hard to get their applause; they could not expect it as a matter of course at the end of each act. Audiences were as likely to hiss or boo if the histrionics had not been up to expectations. The great Georgian actor, David Garrick, sometimes employed 'hush-men' in the audience who would signal the need for silence as he approached some of his more tragic scenes. It was not unknown for actors to stop and ask the audience for help in stopping the noise from a particular box or person.[65]

The poorer people in the gallery, many of whom came into the theatre on half-price tickets near the end of the first play, were the worst behaved and noisiest and the most in need of placating by the actors, hence the expression of 'playing to the gallery'. They did not, though, have a monopoly on the bad behaviour, particularly not when drink was involved. At a benefit performance for Mr Brunton in 1793, it was reported that the audience's attention to the farce:

> was interrupted by the intrusion of a few votaries to Bacchus, whose gallant behaviour caused such an overflow in the boxes that several ladies were obliged to leap into the pit, to escape the fury of these pot valiant heros.[66]

Interestingly, the drinking was not just a problem in front of the curtain. In 1795, the paper complained that the merits of one of the plays had been confounded and obscured by

Mr Sloman who did not sing a song

Mrs Sloman

50

'a tumult that prevailed during a whole performance' caused by 'a joyous set of gentlemen behind the scenes'.[67] Backstage staff during this period were often accused of not being aware that they needed to do their part to help the audience suspend their disbelief. In his memoirs, Charles Matthews recalled the occasion when a stagehand went nonchalantly on stage to give Mrs Siddons a glass of ale while she was in the middle of her Lady Macbeth sleepwalking scene.

There are no detailed records of audience sizes. For most of the period covered by this chapter, however, numbers seem to have fluctuated just above or below the numbers needed for profitability. There were notable exceptions when the theatre could be packed full, such as on the visit of Eliza O'Neill, and others when it was practically empty as it was for performances of *The Heir at Law* and *Of Age To-morrow* in 1812, which, according to a letter from Lady Bolingbroke:

> were performed to an audience of two ladies with silver tickets and two little boys, one little boy in the gallery, who, frightened at being alone, ran away, two persons in the pit, and three in the lower boxes.[68]

Audience numbers dropped to low levels in the 1820s as the original theatre building became increasingly dilapidated. In February 1823, a production of *The Merchant of Venice* was played out before an almost empty theatre with 'not a single person in the pit'. However, some of the empty seats were filled when the half-price crowd came in to see the melodrama *The Two Galley Slaves,* a piece dismissed by the *Chronicle* as a totally unworthy parody that was coarse, low, and 'meager in wit and lame in metre'.

The Norwich Company continued to present a blend of Shakespeare, classical and contemporary plays throughout the period. There was a notable increase in the number of historical and patriotic plays that were presented during the wars with France round the turn of the century. Gothic horror plays such as 'Monk' Lewis's *Castle Spectre* turned up more frequently on the playbills in the later part of the 18th century. And round the turn of the century, performances increasingly ended with a melodrama rather than a farce. Among the most popular melodramas were *The Miller and his Men, The Dog of Montargis, The Dumb Ward of Genoa, The Bleeding Nun of Lindenberg,* and *Timour the Tartar*. In deciding how many melodramas to produce, the management had to balance their enormous attraction to the gallery against the disapprobation of the more discriminating public in the boxes. This is a challenge that managers of commercial theatre have confronted ever since. The dilemma was well summed up in an article in the *Norfolk Chronicle* in 1823:

> We regret to say that the depravity of public taste in histrionic representations has driven and still continues to drive from the stage the sterling works of the old masters, and to re-ceive in their stead the tawdry tinsel stuff of modern composition. The legitimate has given way to a spurious drama, which is as despicable as it is ridiculous – a thing of much sound and little sense.[69]

Concerns about audience sizes and the increasingly-dilapidated state of the building contributed to a malaise at the Theatre Royal in the early 1820s. William Wilkins, the manager, felt that it could only be remedied by the construction of a new and better building.

To conclude with the Melo-Drame of

Raymond and Agnes;

OR THE

Bleeding Nun of Lindenberg.

Don Raymond, Mr. VINING——Don Felix, Mr. CLIFFORD
Baron Lindenberg, Mr. POWELL
Theodore, Mr. FAUCIT———Baptista, Mr. BEACHEM
Claude, Mr. H. VINING
Conrad, Mr. MORELAND———Robert, Mr. BIRRELL
Jaques, Mr. HEWETT—Landlord, Mr. GREEN

Agnes, Miss DIDDEAR———Cunegonde, Mrs. JONES
Marguerette, Mrs. FAUCIT
Baroness Lindenberg, Mrs. CLIFFORD—Bleeding Nun, Miss JONES
Ursula, Mrs. FITZGERALD

Tickets may be had of Mr. H. Vining, at Mrs. Church's, Chapel-field;
and of Miss Tubby at the Theatre, where places for the boxes may be
taken.   [*C. Berry, jun. Printer.*].

A playbill for Raymond and Agnes or The Bleeding Nun of Lindenberg

Chapter 5

1825 - 1885: The Victorian Period

The early Victorian period was not a generally happy one for the Theatre Royal, or, indeed, for Norwich. After the golden period of the late 18th century, Norwich entered into a period of serious economic decline.

Victorian Norwich

The population figures reflect what was happening in the Norwich economy. In 1752, the city had a population of about 36,000. Fifty years later (by the night of the 1801 census) the figure had risen by about 5000 to 41,764, suggesting a net increase of only about 100 people per year. In contrast, in the ten-year period between 1821 and 1831, census figures suggest an annual net increase of over 1000 people each year.[70] Almost all the migrants were poor agricultural labourers moving in from the surrounding countryside. The combined effects of the agricultural depression that followed the Napoleonic Wars and the introduction of new steam-powered threshing machines meant that wages and employment in the rural areas were contracting sharply. Norwich proved to be a magnet because it offered better chances of finding casual labour, slightly more generous poor relief, and - in the minds of some - better opportunities for thieving. Crime rates in Norwich rose sharply in the early years of the 19th century, as did public floggings and other punishments. The influx of poor labourers' families from the countryside in the 1820s was accompanied by falling wages and employment in the city's principal industry - weaving.

The weavers - who had already lost foreign markets during the wars - now faced increasing competition from manufacturers of cotton and silk goods. And, finally, it was obvious that working on individual looms could never be as productive as working on the industrial looms that were going into operation elsewhere in the country. A reduction in the weavers' remuneration in 1829 triggered a wave of protests that included vandalising employers' property and violence against 'scabs'. One observer wrote in 1830 that 'want and wretchedness, and ruin surround us on every side'[71] To make matters worse for the weavers, the wages for alternative forms of employment were also falling because of the plentiful supply of cheap labour freshly arrived from the countryside.

By the mid-19th century, Norwich was a 'down-at-heel' city with growing areas of newly-built slums. The foul-smelling river Wensum meandered slowly through the city carrying away not only industrial waste but the effluent of 20 sewers. There were recurring outbreaks of cholera with major epidemics in 1831-32, 1848-49 and 1853-54. At Christmas 1840, the *Norwich Mercury* reported 'never on any former occasion have the poor been brought to the condition of squalid poverty which now pervades almost all their destitute and comfortless habitations'. Some eight years later, about 20 per cent of the population were not merely poor but paupers surviving either in the workhouse or on poor relief barely sufficient to fend off starvation.

The second Theatre Royal building

The theatre had undergone major rebuilding in 1801 and several renovations in the years that followed. By 1817, William Wilkins was calling for another series of major renovations. However, there was a limit to what could be done with the building, as it was not really possible to expand the space for performers or audience. Moreover, the costs of maintaining the old building were high. In 1819, one writer noted, that 'the demolition and re-erection of the theatre is ... said to be in agitation'.

After his father's death, William Wilkins Junior continued to push for a new building. Plans were finally approved in April 1825 and the new theatre was built just a few feet to the west of the old one and on the same site as the present theatre. It took less than a year to erect and construction costs came to about £6000 (around £350,000 in 2007 terms). In Wilkins' words, he replaced a 'ruinous old barn' with what was described as an 'elegant and substantial new building'. (Thomas Ivory has the reputation of being Norwich's greatest architect and builder of the 18th century and indeed many of his buildings such as the Octagon Chapel still stand today. The original Theatre Royal building seems to have been one of his least-successful endeavours. Given the financial uncertainties surrounding its construction, perhaps the budget had, simply, been too low.)

Wilkins did not demolish the old Theatre Royal building at the same time as he was putting up the new one, thinking he could sell it (for some non-theatrical use) and defray some of the costs. He wasn't successful though. Four years later, the *Norfolk Chronicle* reported that part of the roof of the old building fell in with a tremendous crash - fortunately after the workers had left for the day.

William Wilkins Junior, 1778-1839
Wilkins was a distinguished architect, one of the leading figures in the English Greek revival of the early 1800s. He was responsible for several famous buildings in both classical neo-Grecian and Gothic styles, notably for the National Gallery in London and several college buildings in London and Cambridge. Closer to home, he built the Theatre Royal, Bury St Edmunds and worked on the reconstruction of the crumbling exterior of Norwich Castle. Like his father, Wilkins loved the theatre and initially was not unduly exercised that the Theatre Royal and the other theatres on the East Anglian circuit were not profitable. At the peak of his career, he was known in Norwich for the lavish entertainment he hosted in the theatre building.

The new theatre opened on Easter Monday 1826. It was more spacious with seating for about one thousand people and the interior was elegant with lines of 'classical purity'.[72] Along the sidewalls were two tiers of spacious boxes and in the body of the theatre there were three levels of seating: the pit at ground-floor level, above that the dress circle and above that the gallery. Some efforts had been made to make the audience more comfortable and every other form-bench in the pit was given a back while the first and second rows in the boxes were stepped. Provisions were made also for the selling of refreshments in the gallery, pit and upper boxes. The following year a request was made for refreshments in the dress circle as well, more specifically for 'a sandwich Tray, bearing all the good things of this life, including segars, &c.'[73]

The theatre was quite colourful. The boxes were lined with a crimson material matching the covering of the benches of the pit. The wall between the lower and upper boxes was covered with French wallpaper showing cupids on a dark-blue background with gold ornamentation. The upper-wall space between the gallery and the upper boxes showed antique figures in gold against a white background bordered above and below by imitation marble.

Inside, at least, it was a handsome building. Even the *Theatrical Observer* (a paper that had a brief life in 1827 and, as will be seen later, was an annoying thorn in the flesh of the Theatre Royal management), acknowledged that the decorations were 'tasteful and neat' and that it was 'perhaps, one of the most elegant buildings as to its internal construction that we behold out of the metropolis'.[74] The scenery also won plaudits: Mr Thorne's new creations were described as 'masterful and beautiful'.[75]

The second Theatre Royal building in 1826

The new theatre was not, however, an unqualified success. The stage was flat rather than gently raked and the seats of those in the pit were not sufficiently raised to command a view of the action on the whole depth of the stage. The *Theatrical Observer* noted that

> in the event of a corps de ballet being ever brought out … the admirers of a well-turned female ancle, may as well be at home, as come here.

The lighting, too, was a disappointment. The lamps themselves were elegant and were designed according to the Argand principle. They produced greater candlepower than the old lamps but they were still not powerful enough and the theatre remained gloomy. The *Norwich Mercury* called on Wilkins to complete 'his beautiful theatre, by illuminating it with oil gas from an apparatus especially attached to the building'. (There was no mains supply of gas in Norwich at this time. Gas lighting would not, in fact, be installed at the theatre for another ten years.)

Argand Lamps In 1784, Ami Argand, a Swiss chemist, came up with the principle of using an oil lamp with a hollow circular wick surrounded by a glass chimney. This improved the combustion of the oil and resulted in a brighter light with less smoke. This kind of lamp required more fuel than conventional oil lamps, but had a significant brightening impact on the lighting in large public places.

The *Theatrical Observer* thought the lamps were an 'abominable mode of lighting' and also 'recommended a gas-fuelled elegant chandelier … suspended from a dome-shaped ceiling'. This, it said, 'would have had a splendid effect, and would have made the theatre appear twice the size it now does'. It also called for the installation of statues supporting Grecian tripod lamps at each side of the stage, the failure to do so, it claimed, reflected 'a degree of niggard parsimony which corrodes and destroys everything it touches'.[76] Theatre lighting in the days before gas and electricity was a labour-intensive affair. All lighting effects were produced by tallow candles and oil lamps and several people were needed to execute the 'lamps-up' and 'lamps-down' directions. There would have been candle-grease drippings on the walls and floors on both sides of the curtain and the smell of so many burning wicks must have been particularly unpleasant for spectators in the boxes closest to the stage. The bad smell was one of the reasons women often went to the theatre with their fans and their 'vinaigrettes' (smelling salts).

One of the justifications for building a new theatre was to make access into and out of the building safer. The new building *was* safer, but not by much. To gain entrance to the pit, patrons had to walk down a dimly-lit passageway and descend a long, narrow flight of steps that was only about four feet wide. At the bottom was the box of the 'check-taker', to whom all spectators had to hand their token. On busy nights, the stairs jammed up and impatient patrons often tried to push through. In the mêlée, people were sometimes pushed 'with great violence against the opposite wall'.[77] In 1843, parts of the audience were trapped in the theatre while a terrific thunderstorm flooded parts of the city including some of the theatre's exits.

The opening night prologue

Immortal Shakespeare! Still thy laurels
   bloom,
Tho' ages roll their shadows o'er thy tomb
Sire of the Drama! - may thy spirit's light
Shed its bright influence on our scene ·
   tonight,
And win the guerdon of a favouring smile
From this fair circle for our new rais'd pile
Thou, whose bold genius on a barbarous
   age
Dispens'd enchantment and refin'd the
   stage
Where painted pageantry, all gay
   bedight,
Rais'd at the best a rabble's rude delight,
Or, to amuse some brain-sick Courtier's
   mind,
Were quaint devices by dull bards
   designed,
And for the flash of wit, bright, sparkling,
   clear,
Crept tortur'd puns, fantastically queer;
Such as the licens'd Fool in office made,
Who look'd with ire on rivals in the trade.
Such was the taste till poesy's pure flame,
And magic charms with thee, O
   Shakespeare came;
Then formal pedantry, dull studied art,
Was chang'd for language glowing from
   the heart;
Intricate allegories yielded place
To passion's stormy strength and touching
   grace:
In nature's simple loveliness attir'd,
All felt the master spirit, and admir'd,
And with contemptuous feelings turned
   away
From the quaint pageants of a darker day.
But not like these the favourite of an hour -
Succeeding ages still admit thy power.
Still, in unrivall'd majesty sublime,
Thy genius conquers language, fashion,
   time;
Yea, all confess it mighty, as when first
O'er Britain's isle its proud refulgence burst.
And oft, and fondly, may thy votaries here
Yield at thy call the ready smile and tear -
Own the alternate throb of rage and woe,
The rush of interest, and the generous glow
Of tender sympathy for injur'd worth,
Call'd by creative fancy into birth;
And in the thrill of mimic passion's strife
Forget the cold realities of life.
To these we consecrate this votive dome,
Wit's scenic temple, and the Muse's home.

The opening night of the new theatre

On Saturday, 25 March 1826, two days before the official opening, Wilkins invited 150 of the great and good of the city to take a look at the completed building. He gathered them in the green room for a 'sumptuous collation', which included 'exhilarating draughts of sparkling champagne' followed by a dance on the stage. Wilkins had high hopes for the future. Anticipating big audiences, he tried to head off any traffic congestion by requesting that carriages drop passengers off at the Chapelfield side and pick them up on the Theatre Plain side. He must have been disappointed when he failed to fill the theatre for the much-advertised opening night on Easter Monday, particularly since there were two popular plays on the programme.

The new theatre opened with a 50-years-old favourite - Richard Brinsley Sheridan's *The School for Scandal.* The star performer was David Webster Osbaldiston, whose performances in Norwich paved the way for his later successes in London. He was a strong actor whose emotional reserve and economy of gesture made him stand out from the histrionic over-actors of his day; he was one of the best examples of the way in which the Norwich Company of Comedians served as a nursery for the London stage.

He went on to manage Covent Garden, Sadler's Wells and Victoria theatres in London and is acknowledged as one of the key players in the development of the domestic melodrama. Probably the only reason he is not better known today is that offers of leading roles dried up after his affair with the actress, Eliza Vincent, brought on him the opprobrium of Victorian society.[78]

As the curtain rose, the company came to the front of the stage and sang God Save the King with vocal variations (roulades and volatas) that were not to the taste of everyone in the audience. Then Osbaldiston stepped forward to deliver an opening address that had been composed by a 'young lady of Suffolk'. It was in homage to Shakespeare and very much in the same style of the opening address delivered for the original theatre building in 1758:

David Osbaldiston as Virginius

If the 'young lady from Suffolk' was in the audience, she might well have been disappointed because Osbaldiston reportedly forgot some of the words and generally made a mess of it. (Perhaps he considered this piece of amateur writing beneath him.) Anyway, he and the company went on to give a strong performance of *The School for Scandal*, despite having to compete with the shouting of 'two or three coxcombs in a state of noisy inebriation'.[79] At some point in the performance, these drunks assaulted the man selling refreshments, knocking him to the floor and beating him and were eventually quieted down by hooting from the gallery. Audience problems like these were to prove an ongoing and frequent irritant for the actors and a costly headache for the management for several decades.

After the closing curtain on the play, one member of the company, Mr Baker, performed a well-received song about the merits of the new theatre. He sang another witty song as an encore. When called out for a second encore, Baker stepped forward and reproved the audience for the 'absurdity of such a demand' and explained 'the impossibility he felt of complying with it'. His attitude demonstrates another dynamic of early 19th-century audiences - the strong sense of dialogue between performer and spectator. After the songs, the evening concluded with William Dimond's 1805 comic opera *Youth Love and Folly*.

The theatre faces difficulties

Wilkins' optimism for the future proved ill founded. Norwich was in economic decline and it proved difficult to attract audiences anywhere near big enough to pay back his investment in the new theatre. As already mentioned, his attempts were not helped by the creation of a weekly Norwich newspaper dedicated to discussions of the Norwich theatre scene, namely the *Theatrical Observer*. Founded by a Dr A. F. Fayerman, the paper borrowed a line from *Othello* to proclaim that it would 'nothing extenuate, nor set down aught in malice'. Fayerman (a medical doctor and a pamphleteer) was a testy and controversial figure, forbidden to treat patients in the hospital and generally shunned by the Norwich medical establishment. In the first issue of his paper in February 1827, he made swingeing attacks on the Theatre Royal's production of *Macbeth*: the acting (Malcolm's army was 'six vilely drilled supernumeraries' and his speech to it 'was a burlesque of what it should have been'); the singing ('the singing throughout this piece (if singing it is called) was the vilest concert in imitation of cats on the house tops in a frosty night's serenade we ever heard'); and stage management ('or rather mismanagement').

The audience was also berated:

> What are the Mayor's offices about that they cannot or will not preserve order in the Gallery and slips. Some person threw half an orange on the stage, which struck Mr Balls on the face on Saturday night (Shame).

There was praise for some good performances but the attack journalism continued throughout the year much to the consternation of the theatre management. Fayerman clearly hated the theatre manager, James 'Jockey' Smith, so called because of his penchant for wearing tight-fitting coats, knee breeches, silk stockings and a white cravat beneath his florid face and heavy wig. Fayerman could not forgive him for being, as he saw it, motivated more by profit than by art and for 'getting-up' plays 'in the most hasty and slovenly manner'. In May 1827, Fayerman was in the audience and took exception to 'four blasphemous oaths' uttered on stage. He stood up at the front of his box and proclaimed his objection. He was then set upon by a group of military officers who tried to eject him from the theatre. Smith then appeared shouting sarcastically: 'Don't hurt him much, because if you do we shall catch it in the *Observer*!' Smith's predictions were, of course, fulfilled. Fayerman regaled readers in the next edition with his account of what had happened and, in particular, the violence he had received at the hands of 'several officers from the Barracks (who are permitted to turn the theatre into a Westminster Pit by smoking and swearing in the dress circle).'

The *Observer*'s objection to the oaths was typical of its condemnation of all that was low-brow. After a dismally-attended performance of Shakespeare's *The Winter's Tale*, the paper expressed dismay that audiences were brought in by 'cheap diversions' like *The Dumb Girl of Genoa* and not 'legitimate' drama. It was a 'puppet-show age' in which 'actresses were driving coarse bargains with their managers for exhibiting their persons to gaping curiosity, after every recent degradation of character' and 'harlotry was flaunted in every box'. Fayerman deplored that instead of leading popular taste, the theatre's management was forever following the 'multitude to do evil'.[80] And then in October, after just 42 issues, the *Observer* stopped publication and disappeared as abruptly as it had come to life. During its brief life, it had called for the performance of classical and intellectually-respectable plays to be performed before respectable and well-behaved audiences. Perhaps the editor finally realised that then - as is the case today - a commercial theatre can only be successful if it provides plays in keeping with the interests and spirit of the time. In the 1820s, this meant including at least some plays with romantic sentimentality, robust humour and sword-rattling patriotism. This fare appealed to the growing popular audience but not to the cultured audience that Fayerman felt he represented.

It soon became clear to Wilkins and his fellow investors that they were going to struggle to recoup their outlays. Audiences were very thin, particularly on cold or wet nights. Sometimes there were less than 100 people in the audience and - instead of the expected profits - the theatre was regularly losing money. The actors continued to receive their base pay but they suffered financially, too. In 1825, the end-of-season benefit performances had raised an average of £86 but by 1828 the figure had sunk to £62. In 1833, one reporter questioned whether the receipts of the house could cover the weekly salary of a single member of the cast. Things had little changed by the 1847 season when the proceeds for December-January and for the summer season were reported as barely adequate to cover salaries. The poor financial results exacerbated a crisis for the theatre. An inventory taken the year before revealed that repairs were needed for floors and seats, skirting-boards, doors and door-cases. What's more, defective brickwork needed taking down and rebuilding and much of the roof slating required repairing or renewing. The whole building, inside and out, needed repainting.[81] In 1847, under heavy financial pressure, the manager Mr T. D. Davenport assaulted a man outside the theatre who was trying to sell some complimentary tickets. Davenport, who was arrested, claimed that over the past 20 years this type of practice had cost the theatre some £6000. The magistrates fined him a nominal sum.

T.D. Davenport - Theatre Royal manager 1846-48

Davenport and Charles Dickens
It is generally held that it was Davenport who turned Charles Dickens down in Portsmouth, when the writer applied to join his company. Davenport told him he would never make an actor. The rejection annoyed Dickens so much, the story goes, that he retaliated by using Davenport as a model for the exaggerated character of Vincent Crummles in *Nicholas Nickleby*. Davenport's daughter, who played at the Theatre Royal, was, probably, the model for the Infant Phenomenon of the Crummles Company.

The theatre's financial woes set up a vicious circle - a decline in revenues led to a decline in the quality of the productions, which led to a further decline in revenues. While there were a few great performances from actors who went on to establish national reputations, there were constant complaints about poor stage management, mismatched costumes, late entries, audible prompts, over-frequent repetition of old plays and under-rehearsed new ones. In 1830, Wilkins had still not recouped his expenditure and petitioned the owners to reduce his rent from £600 per year to £400. The owners agreed 'to meet the present depression of the times'. Wilkins never realised his financial hopes for the theatre and after his death, his son confided that his earnest wish was 'to be quit of a concern that harassed his life out'. The finances of the theatre reached their nadir in the mid-1840s when members of the acting company were forced to accept a 25 per cent reduction in their wages. On 26 July 1845, George Smith, who had been the manager for six years, resigned and told the audience: 'This evening brings my disastrous campaign to its close.' Soon after his departure, the old Norwich Company of Comedians was disbanded and the manager set up a new more flexible (and thus cheaper) touring group not bound by a contract. The financial problems suffered by the Theatre Royal were widespread. Indeed, many provincial theatres throughout the country had to close down. What likely saved the Theatre Royal was that between the 1820s and 1850s no businessman who could have converted it to another use wanted to buy it.

Visiting stars

Stars from the London stage were regularly brought in to boost audience numbers. The strategy generally succeeded, but the stars' wages and expenses incurred bringing them to Norwich meant that the theatre often earned no more than it did staging the less-popular, home-grown productions. There were also occasions when even the London stars could not attract Norwich people out to the theatre. Recalling his trip to the city in 1835, William Macready wrote:

William Macready as Shylock

I might find an excuse to my inability to excite the audience in the difficulty of ascertaining where the audience was.[82]

Edmund Kean returned to Norwich to give a farewell appearance before his trip to America and his retirement. He arrived only a couple of hours before the opening-night curtain and his fatigue was evident in a lacklustre performance of Richard III. Fortunately, he picked up and gave strong performances of Shylock and Othello later in the week. But he knew he was not the performer he had been and confided as much to the audience after his final performance:

My labours not only for the past 6 nights, but for the last 3 weeks, have left me in such a state of exhaustion that in the concluding scene this evening I was not confident of being worthy to receive your approbation...[83]

His son, Charles, also played in Norwich as did Fanny Kemble, Madame Vestris, Madame Celeste and John Sheridan Knowles, as well as other well-known names of the 19th-century theatre.

William Macready - who was well known for the vigour with which he attacked his roles - visited the city on three occasions. One night in Norwich in 1828, acting the part of Virginius, he almost throttled John Smith, the manager's son, who was playing Marcus. Smith felt he had to protect himself for the next performance.

> So, having more regard for personal comfort than histrionic effect and secure in his position as the manager's son, he appeared in the throttling scene with a great wad of cotton wool and towelling around his neck under the toga, infinitely to Macready's dismay and a measureless indignation.[84]

Madame Celeste and Madame Vestris often played the roles of men, the so-called breeches parts. This allowed them to display their shapely legs, arms and shoulders uncovered and to wear close-fitting costumes that defined the other attractive parts of their anatomy that 19th-century female fashion resolutely covered up. No doubt, the management hoped that the acting skills of these Mesdames would attract the customers. It also, no doubt, hoped that they would attract local men who were not regular attenders by providing them with opportunities to study female anatomy that were otherwise quite rare in Victorian times. The picture of Madame Celeste is from *The French Spy*, a melodrama in which she played the roles of a refined French lady, a dashing cadet of the Lancers (the spy of the title) and an Arab boy who performed a 'wild' dance that unfailingly brought down the house.

Animal shows were introduced in 1838 with the appearance of Andrew Ducrow's Equestrian Company, which included a 'hippo-dramatic spectacle of St George and the Dragon' and also a version of *Timour the Tartar* with performing horses.

Ducrow returned several times. When he presented his dramatic piece, *Bull Fight,* in 1842, the management had to reassure potentially-nervous patrons that the bull wasn't real but a trained horse 'encased in a bull's hide'.

Madame Vestris who appeared at the Theatre Royal in 1829. She is pictured here playing Don Giovanni.

Andrew Ducrow

The Bull Fight – not for nervous patrons

In addition to the famous actors, there were also visits from composer-musicians Niccolo Paganini and Franz Liszt and from entertainers such as The Great Blondin, the tightrope walker, and 'General' Tom Thumb, who attracted large audiences during his visit in July 1844, towards the middle of his first European tour. In 1866, Tom Thumb made a return trip to the Theatre Royal, which ended in tragedy. Performing with his wife, Lavinia - who was even shorter than him - and with a young baby, the act was billed as 'General Tom Thumb and his celebrated little wife together with their infant daughter, the wonder of the age'. Their act blended elements of comedy, song and dance and about halfway through the act (to great applause) Lavinia brought the baby on the stage and presented her to the audience. While they were in Norwich the child fell ill and had to be left with a nurse at the Norfolk Hotel in St Giles' Street, while General and Mrs Thumb went off to

General Tom Thumb and his wife Lavinia

General Tom Thumb

Tom Thumb, born Charles Stratton in Connecticut in the United States in 1838, was a 'dwarf'. At the age of four, when he was only 24 inches tall, the circus impresario P. T. Barnum discovered him and exhibited him in a freak-show in New York. Barnum noticed that the boy was intelligent and could earn him more money as a bona-fide performer than as a static exhibit. He trained him in acting, mimicking, singing and dancing and ushered in the character of General Tom Thumb. He then sent him on a three-year European tour during which he was received by Queen Victoria and several other royal families and became internationally famous.

Great Yarmouth and Lowestoft. In their absence, the child's condition deteriorated and she developed an 'inflammation of the brain'. Despite the best efforts of the doctors (Dr Holland and Mr Crawford-Bell), there was no recovery. Lavinia was called back to Norwich and 'remained in attendance on the little patient till death put an end to its sufferings'. The baby was buried at the Norwich cemetery before a large crowd of local people on 26 September with the Rev Mr Wortley (of St Gregory's) officiating.[85] However, unknown to the mourners, General and Mrs Thumb were, in fact, childless. The baby being buried that day had been borrowed from a foundling home as a means of increasing interest in their act.

The struggle to attract audiences

To swell audience figures, the management in the early years of the new Theatre Royal still advertised performances, particularly of Shakespearian plays, where the lead role would be taken by a local 'gentleman' - perhaps a precursor of today's reality TV where minor celebrities are humiliated before an audience. As the *Theatrical Observer* noted of an 1827 performance of *Romeo and Juliet* in which the young gentleman had played the title role as a 'rude robust strapping sort of boatswain':

> It is really astonishing to see how masses of people are drawn together by insatiate curiosity, when an honourable or right honourable shall deign to step out of the usual sphere of high life, and put themselves on their trial before the tribunal of the people.

The management attempted to drum-up ticket sales by offering increasingly low-brow material including flimsy comic operas and burlettas and Gothic chillers such as *The Bleeding Nun of Lindenberg*. The playbills became noticeably more flamboyant and aimed at an audience wanting exciting entertainment rather than intellectual reflection. One playbill in 1833 announced *Giovanni in London: or the Libertine Reclaimed* as a

> comic extravaganza entertainment in 2 acts comprising a grand choral, satirical, tragical, comical, operatical, melodramatical, pantomimical, critical, infernal, terestrial, celestial, one word in all -gullymaufricalollapadrical burletta spectacle.

The struggle to sell tickets to the new Theatre Royal was made difficult not only by the depressed economic conditions of the early- to mid-19th century but also by the growing competition in the local entertainment industry. The Adelphi Theatre in Ranelagh Gardens (close to the site of the present-day city-centre store of Sainsburys) was a particular rival. It presented plays with a local interest such as *Ethelrida, Princess of Norwich, King of Mercia and East Anglia and the Wild Woman of Mosswold Heath* and *The Spirit of the Loom*. The Theatre Royal management tried to persuade the local magistrates that they should refuse the Adelphi a license on the grounds that the theatre was 'immoral in the highest degree' and an influence for 'dissipation and vice'. Later, there was competition from the music halls, particularly from the Vaudeville Theatre in St Giles' Street housed on the site of the present Salvation Army Citadel. Several inns and taverns in the city also competed for the people's shrinking entertainment budget by mounting musical entertainment, puppet shows and - a speciality of the Angel Inn in the market place -circus-type acts - the more bizarre the better! Nothing at the Angel, though, could match the act closed down by the mayor at the 1863 Christmas fair where a man and a woman 'said to be Kaffirs' pulled in the crowds by eating live rats.[86]

The Theatre Royal management faced a dilemma. The more they 'marketed' their productions to the gentle, better-educated and better-off parts of the local population the less they appealed to the less sophisticated, less well-educated and less well-off parts of the population. Of course, some of the gentle parts of the population probably found the noise and banter of the gallery rather exciting and many of the poorer parts of the population, no doubt, liked to feel a part of the same audience as the local 'quality'. However, it is clear that during its first 50 years or so the management of the new Theatre Royal felt like they had to choose between one market and the other. On most occasions they bowed to popularity. In March 1858 the *Chronicle* reported:

> During the past three weeks Mr Sidney has attempted to attract audiences by resorting to a succession of 'stars', but he has failed, except so far as the pit and the gallery are concerned…the great vice of a purely gallery and pit attendance is the noise and disgusting language which frequently annoys ears not accustomed to such ebullitions of coarseness.[87]

The Mr Sidney referred to was William Sidney who had taken over the management of the theatre in 1854. He had been associated with it for more than three decades as had his wife and two daughters. He had appeared frequently on stage, particularly in his signature role as Rip Van Winkle. Sidney later became a lessee and the majority shareholder.

He, too, experienced great difficulty in attracting a more-refined audience to the theatre. One reason for this was that the coming of the railways in the mid-1840s gave better-off people more opportunities of travelling down to London for their entertainment.[88] Another reason was the growing strength of prudishness and moral fundamentalism now referred to as Victorian values. The reviewer in the *Norfolk Chronicle* exemplified these views. In 1829, he criticised the theatre for putting on a strongman act on the grounds that the performer's bare torso was 'more fitted for the sculptor to contemplate in a studio than on the stage of a theatre'.[89] In an 1833 review, Madame Celeste was criticised for exerting 'herself somewhat too much in the pirouette, considering the proximity of spectators in a provincial theatre to the stage'.[90]

William Sidney, Theatre Royal manager 1854-85

Several years later (in 1872) the reviewer told the theatre manager that by putting on the French play, *Frou Frou or Fashion and Passion*, he

> must be little acquainted with the character of the respectable portion of the playgoers of this city in supposing that to such a play they will take either their wives or their families.

A final reason for the difficulty in attracting a quality audience was that, as the years passed with few profits made, the theatre building had become shabby. As the *Norwich Mercury* commented:

> various circumstances have contributed to repulse the better classes, except on particular occasions … [S]ome of old taste might be revived … if the boxes and seats were neat, cleanly and in tolerably decent repair…[A]t any rate no place of public amusement could be more miserable and wretched in this respect.[91]

Whatever the causes, as one reporter noted in 1845, the 'aristocracy have apparently taken a distaste to the theatre, which nothing can overcome'.

Madame Céleste over-exerting herself in a pirouette

Norwich audiences in the Victorian years

The typical Theatre Royal audience of this period had thus changed from its Georgian counterpart. The gentle people no longer came to the theatre to be seen. But the audience was still noisy and interactive. It would hiss not only at the entry of villains but also at forgotten lines or other problems on stage and would not hesitate to call out their advice to the manager or the players. Harcourt Bosworth in the compilation of his memories of the Theatre Royal remembered back to one night in the 1850s when the audience in the gallery was particularly vocal. The curtain dropped on *The Merchant of Venice* at the end of the fourth act and the band began to play and carried on for much longer than was usual between acts. When the curtain came up it revealed not Portia's residence but a modern cottage. The actors were in modern costumes and their opening dialogue was patently not Shakespearian.

> Then the 'gods' woke -up. Whistles, cat calls, yells, and every one of the numerous methods of disapprobation these exalted personages can employ.

The actors could not be heard and after a few minutes, the manager, Joseph Clarence, overcoat on and hat in hand, rushed on to the stage and - 'looking a whole armoury of weapons at the noisy gods' - inquired

Gentlemen of the gallery, what is it you want?

The reply was immediate:

The Marchant o' Wenus a'got five acts, and we ain't had only four on 'em.

This was followed by general laughter that even the irate Clarence joined in. He explained that the printer had made a blunder and that the playbills should have announced that the play would terminate with the fourth act that night. He offered his deep apologies for the mistake and appealed to the goodwill of the gallery to let the programme continue.

This explanation being graciously deemed satisfactory by the Shakespearian students aloft, Mr Clarence bowed himself off, and, this pretty interlude being over, the other farce on the bill was then allowed to proceed.

This story illustrates not only the interactivity of those in front of and those behind the curtain but a number of other points, for example, that the company saw nothing unusual in putting on a Shakespeare play without its final act or in having a band play between acts.

The manager referred to was Joseph Clarence (also known as Clarence Holt). He achieved fame in the London music halls impersonating Shakespearian characters. Once a robust actor of the old school with a commanding presence, notably in the role of Richelieu, he took over the manager's job for four years from 1849. His tenure was remembered particularly for his pantomime productions, which were more elaborate and spectacular than anything seen in Norwich before.

William Sidney (the manager in 1862) had to face a similar audience revolt. One

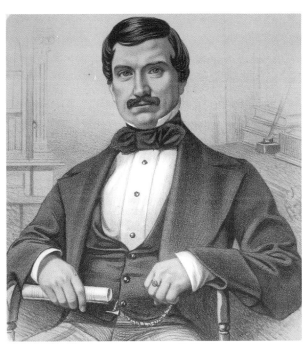

Clarence Holt, Theatre Royal manager 1849-53

night after the conclusion of the main play, he had to go on stage and announce that, because the orchestra leader had been called away, the advertised melodrama would be replaced by a farce. The gallery greeted this announcement with loud groans and hisses. The melodrama, *Nick of the Woods,* was a bloodthirsty piece that was a particular favourite of the patrons up in the gods. A comic song was then performed that was barely audible over the hubbub. When the curtain opened for the farce, the heckling, shouting and hissing reverberated round the theatre. Those in the gallery started throwing orange peel and nutshells down on the spectators in the pit, who, in turn, threw them back. Obviously, none of the actors could be heard above the din. The manager reappeared to appeal for calm but had to retreat before the shouts of 'Give us our money back', 'We have been swindled' and 'Go home to bed'. Mr Cox was then pushed on stage to sing another comic song, but the orchestra refused to accompany him on the grounds that they would play only what they had been engaged to play. The manager again tried addressing the troublemakers as 'gentlemen' and appealing to them for the 'generosity of the British public'. Finally, the farce was allowed to proceed but against a background of constant heckling. To add to the confusion when the uproar was at its worst, the lighting faded as the gas started burning low.

The protests on this occasion seem to have been relatively good-humoured, but on numerous occasions the press reported incidences of appalling audience behaviour. The noise and the assault on opening night and the fracas involving the editor of the *Theatrical Observer* a year later have already been described. In 1832, the *Norfolk Chronicle* reported that,

> the house exhibited some score or two of the most disorderly and drunken fellows that had been introduced, through resources not their own, into a theatre seldom, if ever, disgraced by the presence of such a rabble rout, to hiss and groan at the objects of general applause and respect.[92]

Three years later, the *Chronicle* reported a potentially-horrifying event when, during the performance, an audience member threw 'a chemical substance capable of ignition in different parts of the theatre'. Despite the offer of a large reward of 20 guineas the culprit was never discovered.[93]

One of the worst evenings of unrest came in 1875. On 17 February of that year, the *Norwich Mercury* reported:

> On Saturday…a party of roughs…commenced an assault upon the globes of the gas burners which surround the double tier of boxes, hurling marbles, 'trotter bones' etc at them till one after the other, all the globes were smashed in the most ruthless manner. Some similar characters in the pit, pretending to be annoyed at the things falling down upon them, commenced to hurl them back to the gallery and upper boxes, thus assisting their friends above in smashing the lamps, and generally annoying the more respectable part of the audience. A set of similar characters took possession of the stage, breaking down one of the iron girders in front of the orchestra, and doing other similar mischief. Others seated themselves upon the front of the dress circle, smoking short pipes and otherwise misconducting themselves. The scene throughout was of a disgraceful character.

The police were called in and arrested one of the most aggressive miscreants, William Pottle of Lakenham. He was sent to prison for 14 days with a further 14 to run consecutively in lieu of costs. The editorial writer expressed the theatre management's dilemma:

> No manager can expect support from the respectable inhabitants of the city while such disreputable scenes are allowed constantly to take place.[94]

A ready supply of projectiles was provided during this period by the 'lank-man' who sold nuts, cakes, oranges and three apples for a penny as well as drinks such as lemonade and ginger beer. Whenever the curtain fell, between plays and even between acts of a play, he would push his way between the rows in the pit, treading on people's coat-tails, knocking off their hats with his basket and sometimes even spurting ginger beer in their faces.[95] The sale of fruit, a staple of the early theatre, was discontinued towards the end of the 19th century. It was at about this time that the unwrapping of sweet papers took over from the sucking of oranges as the main noise irritant for those wanting to concentrate on the action on stage.

Most audience problems came in the latter part of the evening's performance after the arrival of the 'half-price' crowd. This practice described earlier continued at the Theatre Royal well into the 19th century. The practice meant that the 'full-price' patrons could be sitting quietly watching, say, a Shakespearian tragedy, until, just before or during the final act, their attention would be shattered by the clattering feet and noisy entrance of spectators, sometimes the worse for drink, who had come for the farce or melodrama. Their entrance was the source of many complaints from both audience members and actors.

Safety at the Theatre Royal

The better-heeled potential theatregoers were certainly put off by these incidences of bad audience behaviour. They were put off just as much by concerns about the security of the theatre building. The Theatre Royal during this period had capacity for an audience of 1000 but as many as 1250 squeezed in on popular nights. The greatest overcrowding was likely to be in the gallery where the city surveyor commented that as many as 400 people had been known to cram into a space designed for a maximum of 300. Even if the audience was below full capacity, it still could not evacuate the building rapidly. Any fire or other mishap requiring an audience evacuation would almost certainly have had fatal consequences. And theatre fires were by no means uncommon. Pantomimes, which tended to attract the largest audiences, were particularly dangerous as special lighting effects often called for gas-jets on different parts of the stage. The gas travelled through rubber tubes that had to be hastily fixed and unfixed to the flammable wood and canvas scenery. All was in close proximity to the performers in their even more flammable gauze and muslin costumes. In 1883, Norwich City Council requested that the management make structural changes to make evacuation easier. The request was given weight by the appalling tragedy at the Victoria Hall in Sunderland in June of that year when children in the gallery had been invited to come downstairs to the stage to receive a present from the performer. Streaming through a bottleneck similar to one at the Norwich Theatre Royal, those in the front got pushed by those behind and 183 were crushed to death.[96] William Sidney (the manager in 1883) had dragged his feet in carrying out the council's request. In one of his communications, he questioned whether the council could require him to take any actions, since, as manager of a patent theatre he came directly under the jurisdiction of the Lord Chamberlain's office and not the local authorities.

When this issue was pursued it revealed that Sidney was wrong and that the Theatre Royal had been operating illegally for over 100 years. Exasperated by Sidney's procrastination, the town clerk of Norwich appealed to the Lord Chamberlain to instruct Mr Sidney to make the necessary changes. The Lord Chamberlain's office responded that the Theatre Royal had received patent status in 1768 and that a license dated 17 March 1768 had been granted to Thomas Ivory to perform stage plays in Norwich between 1 November and the last day of May each year and for a further three weeks in the summer including the week in which the Assizes were held. However, the license had been made personally to Thomas Ivory and could not be passed on after his death. The Norwich Theatre Royal was no longer a patent theatre and was not under the Lord Chamberlain's jurisdiction. In other words, it had been operating unlicensed (and thus illegally) for over 100 years. In fact, the Drury Lane and Covent Garden theatres, which had been granted perpetual patents, were the only two patent theatres in the country; the system of patents granted by the Lord Chamberlain to other theatres had been discontinued. In the case of Norwich Theatre Royal, the city magistrates should have taken over jurisdiction from the time of Ivory's death in 1779.[97] With this information, the city council returned to press Sidney on safety issues and the required changes were made in 1885.

(Interestingly, Burley and others who have written of the history of the Theatre Royal have made much of this revelation. However, the question of whether the theatre had a patent had been discussed some 40 years earlier. In the Norfolk County Record Office there is an 1847 letter from a member of the Wilkins family expressing the opinion that there was no patent and that 'the house was merely opened under the Lord Chamberlain's office'.)[98]

The dangers facing the audiences at the Theatre Royal were greater for the actors, who worked nightly amid naked gas flames and potentially-dangerous scenery. In 1851, Fred Phillips (a rather heavy man) was playing Macgregor in the play *Rob Roy*. In act II, he walked over a bridge that had not been properly built and it gave way. He fell and suffered a bad compound fracture of his leg and was taken to the Norfolk and Norwich Hospital where he remained for several weeks. The surgeons decided to amputate the lower part of his limb. The operation took place without anaesthetic and was 'borne with heroic fortitude by the poor sufferer'.[99] (His doctor, Mr Peter Nicholls, used to refer to his patient as Richard III.) His colleagues rallied round and put on two benefit performances for him and he retired from the stage to become the landlord of the Boar's Head Inn in Norwich's Surrey Street.

In 1866, Louisa Ritter was performing in *The Rose of Ettrick Vale* and one of the scenes included a fire on the stage. Her dress came too near the flame and caught fire. She ran from the stage in terror and managed to ignite some pieces of scenery on her way. She was grabbed, pushed down to the floor and rolled over and over until the flames were extinguished.[100] Even putting on costumes could be hazardous. In 1845, Mrs Bartlett ran a pin into 'one of the arteries of her head' and had to withdraw from the play immediately to get treatment.

There were also dangers from untrustworthy colleagues. In 1871, Mr Strange was playing Harlequin in the pantomime and, in one scene, was supposed to leap from the stage into the arms of a stagehand waiting in the wings. One night, the stagehand got drunk and failed to take up his position and Mr Strange ended up, not surprisingly, in the Norfolk and Norwich Hospital - fortunately without the career-ending injuries received by Fred Phillips. The actors were, in fact, often let down by the backstage crew. The sceneshifters, in particular, often missed their cues and were hissed by the audience

Children on stage

Actors' lives were often made difficult by children who ran round the backstage area getting in the way. Such was the case in an incident that happened in April 1848. As the curtain came down on the first play, the audience heard a large thud and screaming. The six-year-old son of the stage carpenter had run off to play in the flies (the area above the stage from which backdrops and scenery are lowered). From there, he had fallen 20 feet down on to the stage, fortunately escaping with only minor bruises.[101] The fall of this little boy did not inconvenience the actors half as much as the baby girl engaged to play the daughter of Cora and Alonzo in *Pizarro*. In one scene, two soldiers were supposed to enter and discover the child sleeping on a bank. As Harcourt Bosworth recalled the incident,

> that is, the child should be sleeping - but this young 'debutante', being swaddled up as tightly as possible to prevent any attempt at locomotion at the wrong moment, was placed on the 'property' bank and awed into semi-quietude by the shaking fist of the mother at the wing…[but the baby's] shrieks could then be heard all over the theatre … Well, these soldiers should take up the sleeping innocent and carry it off, but this young 'actress' determined on a very different reading of the part, and managed by a supreme struggle to get free from her shawl bindings, and tottered with shrieks and tears to her ag-onised and 'fist-shaking' mother …

But this was not the end of it because the baby plays an integral part in the plot and has to reappear in the next scene,

> where the noble Rolla pleads for the infant's life with these words to the tyrant Pizarro, 'Couldst thou hurt that innocent? By heaven, 'tis smiling in thy face.' Was it? If the most fearful yells ever emitted from childhood's lungs, or the writhings of every limb to get free and toddle off, were signs of contentedness in a happy child, then that budding ac-tress was indeed supremely so. I can't remember how the scene ended. I can only hear the roars of laughter from the amused audience.[102]

The end of the Norwich Company of Comedians

Being part of a stock company, actors in the Norwich Company of Comedians were on stage every week throughout the season and became well-known local figures. As with celebrities today, any scandalous story about one of their members was eagerly received by the local population. No story came much bigger than the elopement of Fanny Vining, the daughter of the company's stars of the moment, Frederick and Marian Vining. Fanny was playing the dutiful daughter Miranda in *The Tempest* at the time when she most undutifully ran away with another (much older) member of the company by the name of Charles Gill.[103] As it turned out, the union did not last long.

The Theatre Royal operated with its own stock company for almost a century. During the 1850s, increasing numbers of performances were presented by travelling companies. By the centennial season in 1858, the old Norwich Company of Comedians had completely disappeared from the Theatre Royal boards. For the management, the switch provided a cut in expenditures and some limitation on financial risk. For the audiences, the benefits were mixed. The stock company allowed audiences a chance to identify with a 'home team' of actors and to share the experience of interpreting different types of material. One of the downfalls of the system, though, was that in having to master so many parts so quickly, the actors lacked time for the reflection and rehearsal needed to turn in great performances. Actors in travelling companies had a limited number of plays in their repertoire, which they played over and over in different towns, thus making possible more polished performances. The practice of engaging travelling theatre companies (generally for a week's run) has been followed by the Theatre Royal management to this day.

The second Theatre Royal building after 60 years

The first 60 years of the new theatre building were not easy ones for either actors or management. Despite many great performances and a few golden patches, it had been a period of decline. Norwich had been passed over by industrialisation and had become a relatively poor city. Quite simply, there weren't enough rich or middling sorts of theatregoers to support a serious theatre. In 1873, one reporter lamented how the Theatre Royal:

> was at one time the 'Actors' School' but of late years has fallen from her high position, and her theatrical taste has sunk so low as to make one almost despair of raising it.

He repeated an often-heard plea for the Theatre Royal management to make greater efforts to win back those who appreciated good acting:

> … to the exclusion of that low class of theatregoers who can never conceive anything more delightful than those plays which border upon vulgarity, and turn every high and noble sentiment to ridicule.

On its 50th anniversary in 1875, the new Theatre Royal was shabby and rundown and 'not creditable to the city'.[104] Many of the more-refined parts of the population were put off going not only by the grime, but also by the smoking and foul language that they found there.[105] On its 60th anniversary, little had changed. Sidney felt he could do no more and handed control over to his assistant, Fred Morgan. Morgan did much to modernise the theatre and improve its image as he took it through into the 20th century.

Chapter 6

1885 - 1925: Into the Twentieth Century

Fred Morgan takes over

Fred Morgan assumed the management of the Theatre Royal in 1885 and with one brief interlude was in charge for thirty years.

Morgan was a strange blend of bombastic showman and personal reticence, making it difficult to distinguish fact from fiction in what he said about himself. Piecing together his story from what people remember him saying gives the following picture. He grew up in Ely, where his father was a Cathedral organist. At some point he must have spent some time with gypsies because there are reports of him speaking the Romany language. He came to Norwich in the 1870s and worked for his uncle who was a chemist in Bedford Street. He went on to open his own chemist shop in Bridewell Alley and became the dispenser for a local doctor. While still a young man, he set off for adventure in Omaha, Nebraska and stayed there with his uncle who was the city postmaster. (The 1870s were the classic days of the Wild West and Omaha on the Missouri river was in the middle of cowboy and Indian territory.) During his time there, he hunted bison and befriended groups of Pawnee Indians. On his return to Norwich, he began to work in theatre. He became assistant manager to Sidney at the Theatre Royal and took over the management of the Connaught Varieties – the music hall in Lower Goat Lane. He had an eclectic circle of friends and acquaintances including: the prize-fighter Jem Mace; the bishop of Norwich, Bishop Sheepshanks (whom he first met as a fellow adventurer during his American stay) and George Borrow, the local author, with whom at one time he probably shared lodgings in a house near the theatre.

Burley recalled him as 'a remarkable man - a wit, prone at times to abruptness, but with a sentimental side to his character which found expression in great tenderness for children'. Morgan liked joking about the life of the theatre. On one occasion, he caused merriment with his description of ladies weeping on their way out of a performance of *East Lynne* and spluttering that they had never enjoyed a play so much.[106] Others remembered a rather sterner figure, who stood at the door of the pit on wet nights shouting 'wipe your feet' at the incoming patrons.[107]

In his first few years in charge, Morgan undertook extensive renovations to the building. Most importantly, he opened up the access ways within the theatre to meet the safety concerns of the city council. These improvements relieved the anxieties of those seated in the pit, which one correspondent had called a 'death-trap'. In a major innovation, he took down the partition between the lower-level boxes (at the rear of the pit) and created rows of seating in an open-plan dress circle, which was freshly painted, re-carpeted and upholstered in dark crimson plush. The rest of the theatre was redecorated and the ceiling was lavishly finished 'a la Parisian Peacock'. In 1894, he took out all the gas fittings and introduced electricity throughout. This brightened up the theatre considerably, greatly improved the stage lighting and opened up possibilities of more dramatic special effects. The switch to electricity had a particularly stunning impact outside the theatre with the installation of a 2900-candle power arc light that must have been one of the brightest light sources in the city.

Programming at the theatre changed significantly but gradually during Morgan's period in charge. At first, the composition of the theatre's yearly programmes was similar to those of his predecessor. During this period, Morgan mostly consolidated the policy changes made by Sidney. Later, he introduced the type of theatrical programming followed today - keeping the theatre open all year round with only a short summer recess and using touring drama companies. Morgan himself acted on a few occasions, but devoted most of his time to making the theatre financially viable.

At the beginning of his management he tried to ensure good-size houses by keeping the standard admission prices at fairly modest levels:

Fred Morgan, Theatre Royal manager 1885-1903, 1904-15

	1885 prices	**(Adjusted by inflation to 2007)**
Circle	3s. 0d.	£10
Upper Boxes	1s. 6d.	£6
Pit	1s. 0d.	£4
Gallery	0s. 6d.	£2

He succeeded in keeping Norwich theatregoers up to date by bringing in some of the best new plays. Musical comedies, which were very popular round the turn of the century, figured frequently in his programmes. This triggered renewed criticisms from those who felt that the theatre should put on well-written thought-provoking plays and not the 'so-called musical comedies' that were without plot and only needed a few catchy, vulgar songs and plenty of high kicking.[108] Although many of the touring companies that came for their week or two in Norwich included nationally-known artists, Morgan failed to bring in the really big names. Whereas in the early 19th century, Edmund Kean and the most famous actors of their day came for short seasons in Norwich, by Morgan's time it became difficult to attract their contemporary counterparts such as Henry Irving, Ellen Terry, Sarah Bernhardt and Max Beerbohm Tree. His difficulties were partly because of an increase in provincial competition - there were more higher-paying, better-equipped and 'less-off-the beaten-track' theatres than there had been a century before.

Nine years after his arrival, Morgan felt that he had made the theatre a safer and more attractive place and that he was attracting a better class of audience. He decided it was time to ask the magistrates to restore the alcoholic drinks license that had been withdrawn from the theatre during the period of disorderly audiences in the 1870s. The application was heard in November 1894 and several things can be learned from the discussion before the magistrates.

- All parties acknowledged that the Theatre Royal before Morgan's arrival had been a 'terrible place' and a 'disgrace to the city' and that improvements had been made.

- The different parts of the auditorium were still divided along lines of social class. Morgan sought a license for patrons of the boxes and circle only. The chairman of the magistrates asked him if he understood correctly: 'you want to supply the better class of people with drink to the exclusion of the poorer people.' Morgan's solicitor spun the answer to this by saying that the bar would only be big enough to serve drinks to these parts of the theatre as there would not be enough room for those in the pit (pittites) or in the gallery (gods). These latter went out between the acts and bought drinks in the pubs close to the theatre, while those in the boxes and circle 'did not care to turn out during the performance, and many of them liked a little refreshment'.

- While audiences were better behaved, Morgan had not entirely succeeded in cutting out incidents of unruliness. On being questioned, he admitted that there 'might have been' a fight in the pit about a month before (but he did not know). He also acknowledged complaints about smoking in the pit and the gallery.

- There was still a link made between the theatre and immorality. One objection to Morgan's application was that selling intoxicated liquors close to the upper boxes "would probably encourage the resort of women". Morgan's application was vigorously opposed by the Sunday School Union and several ministers of religion who argued that a license would be 'dangerous' for the young people of the city.

- The fact that local publicans joined forces in opposition with the churches indicates that a good number of theatre patrons slipped out for a drink during theatre performances - certainly enough to constitute a drinking market worth fighting to protect.

The opposition proved too strong for Morgan and on a majority vote the magistrates turned his application down.

Morgan sells the Theatre Royal

The reputation of the Theatre Royal as a run-down and out-of-date establishment died hard. In the late 1890s a syndicate of investors grouped together to build a more modern theatre and purchased land on St Giles' Street a few yards up from the Guildhall and market place on the site that is now the St Giles' Street multi-storey car park. They had it cleared and started work on the foundations, but no more. The site remained vacant for several years and then was put up for sale in 1902. Fred Morgan got together the finance to build the new theatre himself. He hired as his architect W. G. R. Sprague, who had built several prestigious theatres in London and around the country including, notably, the Lyceum in Sheffield. Sprague designed a building that was not so grand as the syndicate had been planning but, nevertheless, one with a better stage and facilities, better acoustics, more seating capacity and more comfort and space for the audience - a theatre much better than the 'tumbledown, draughty, old building in Theatre Street'.[109]

As work started, Morgan put the old Theatre Royal building up for sale, renewing fears it would disappear. The theatre's supporters were worried that the building would be bought and converted into a vulgar music hall or, even worse, gutted and turned into another shoe factory or church.[110] The building was finally sold to theatre entrepreneurs E. H. Bostock and F. W. Fitt who prepared to reopen it as a venue for twice-nightly variety shows.

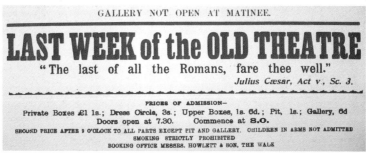

The playbill announcing Morgan's departure

On 3 August 1903, Morgan walked away from the Theatre Royal where he had been manager for 18 years and part of the management team for much longer and presided over the opening night of his new theatre, ostentatiously called the Grand Opera House. He took with him most of his staff. The building was quite 'grand' with four levels of seating - all proper seats, no backless benches as at the Theatre Royal - and ornate decorations. Morgan appears to have been pleased with his venture and is remembered in the winter months standing with his back to the fire in the spacious foyer welcoming the patrons.

The Grand Opera House - a George Swain photograph

Inside the Grand Opera House - a George Swain photograph

Back on Theatre Street, Bostock and Fitt were working out their strategy for the Theatre Royal. One of their first decisions was to 'rebrand' the building by changing its name to the Norwich Hippodrome. Their opening night (31 August) came four weeks later than Morgan's. Before the first performance, a small crowd gathered 'outside the brilliantly-lighted building' to watch the arrival of the wealthy and local-celebrity 'first-nighters'. 'There was a general scene of animation within the vicinity throughout the evening,' which began with the national anthem (sung by local man Harry Haylett) and continued with a somewhat condescending address from the Lord Mayor:

> There are times when to be amused without being called upon to think proves the highest form of enjoyment and it is to provide the citizens with a full opportunity of obtaining this that the new Hippodrome has been opened…I welcome any form of healthy recreation which will draw young people from the streets and provide proper occupation for their spare hours. I am glad to be assured that every possible care will be taken to provide a programme of a high standard and absolutely devoid of anything likely to offend the most exacting requirements [cheers].[111]

The bill for that night was:

Captain Frank Taylor's educated elephants, pony and dogs

Walter Coram, ventriloquist

Wal Robins, black-and-white musical comedian

Clarice Raynor, of the Royal Academy of Music, a singer with a phenomenal voice ('Rocked in the Cradle of the Deep')

The Colberg Family, musical act

The Brothers Artois, horizontal bar

Hess & Lisbon, fancy trick and comedy skaters

Bonnie Goodwin and her Apollo Picaninnies

Captain Taylor (at the top of the bill) was proclaimed to be an 'expensive engagement direct from the Empire Theatre, London'. The local paper noted that the rest of the acts fulfilled to the letter the 'promise of the proprietors that nothing should be included in their performance that was calculated to offend a proper taste'. Not a conclusion that would be drawn today considering the appearance on the programme of Bonnie Goodwin and her Apollo Picaninnies, 'a troupe of young darkies that sing and dance in their native style'.

On some evenings the variety acts were supplemented by 'animated pictures' with titles such as *The Turnout of the Norwich Fire Brigade*. Crude movies of local scenes were extremely popular, too, particularly if there was a chance for audience members to see themselves. Technology had moved on greatly since the days when the theatre had shown 'dissolvent views' powered by oil lamps. These very early silent movies could be inserted or dropped according to how closely the acts were running to their allotted timetable.

One debated question is whether Charlie Chaplin appeared there during the 1904 season. Certainly, the Eight Lancashire Lads (a clog-dancing act) were on the bill for 26 September 1904. This was the troupe that Chaplin had joined as a ten-year-old in 1899 and in which he overlapped at some point with Stan Laurel. But was Chaplin among their number on that night? When in the 1950s he was asked whether he had played with the Lancashire Lads on their appearance in June 1906, he responded that he could not recall doing so but that he could recall performing with them in Norwich at an earlier date.[112] It was deduced that this must have been a reference to his performing on the September 1904 date. However, it is most improbable that he did. Around this time, Chaplin was playing in a touring production of *Sherlock Holmes*. His memory of playing in Norwich probably dates back to the 1899-1903 period and to one of the Lads' performances in George Gilbert's circuses at the Agricultural Hall (presently occupied by Anglia Television at the top of Prince of Wales Road).

Morgan returns

After his first year over at the Grand Opera House, Morgan realised that he would probably never make his new theatre financially viable nor, indeed, earn back the money he had invested in it. He was obliged to sell and advertised it in the *Era*.

> **To Theatre and Music Hall Proprietors and others**
> **WANTED,** to sell by private treaty, magnificent new freehold theatre in first-class provincial town with full dramatic and excise license.
> The building has only been completed twelve months, is fire resisting, and built on the latest principles of steel and concrete. Decorated, fitted, and furnished throughout, including electric lighting, heating and all modern improvements.
> Responsible purchasers or their solicitors only negotiated with
> Apply to
> W.G.R.Sprague, Architect
> Criterion Chambers, 10 and 11 Jermyn Street SW
> Silence a polite negative

The advert obviously referred to Morgan's Grand Opera House and Fitt and his partner, Bostock, stepped in quickly to purchase it. They intended to convert it to a 'Hippodrome and Theatre of Varieties' and transfer there the variety programmes they had for the past year been successfully presenting in the old Theatre Royal building. Fitt explained that when he and his partner had seen the advert for the Opera House, they felt the need to act quickly. If someone else had bought it and started to run variety it would have killed their venture at the much-smaller Hippodrome - the former Theatre Royal. They approached Morgan and in negotiations that were conducted in a spirit 'of the utmost friendliness and good feeling' offered him a deal that Fitt explained might not have been all that Morgan could have wished - but 'this life is one of business'. Bostock and Fitt gave Morgan the first opportunity of taking a lease of the old theatre and turned down offers of £3 or £4 more per week made by other potential managers. Rather patronisingly, Fitt explained:

> My partner has a sympathetic feeling for other people engaged in the same line of business; and he at once declared that Mr Morgan was not to be crushed, but was to be given the preference…while we have the opportunity of allowing Mr Morgan to remain at the old Theatre Royal we shall most certainly do so.[113]

The suggestion that the parties were not the best of friends is supported by disparaging references to Morgan in Mrs Fitt's diary for 1927.[114]

So the Norwich Hippodrome became once again the Theatre Royal and the Grand Opera House (at which no opera had ever been staged) became the new Hippodrome. While local commentators were pleased to see the Theatre Royal take up its historic role once again, many were depressed that Morgan's dream of presenting drama in a new and better-equipped building had been shattered. Morgan took the theatre:

> from a back street and set it on one of the city's chief highways confident that the public would reward the enterprise. They have failed to do so, with the result that the drama retires to relight her torch in the secluded street from whence she came.[115]

Morgan made a considerable financial loss but, according to the local paper, was 'not unduly cast down. He is of a cork-like disposition, with something of the player's happy knack of seeing all the world as a stage.'

In an interview Morgan explained where he thought he had gone wrong. It was not that interest in drama was declining in Norwich; it was stronger than it had been ten years before. Nor was it the case that variety was 'knocking theatre proper into a cocked hat'. Morgan's essential problem was that he could not provide high-class theatrical entertainment in his new building at prices that could compete with those charged at the Hippodrome (the old Theatre Royal building). A man could take his wife and four children to the best places at the Hippodrome for about a third of what the equivalent seating would cost at the Opera House. Moreover, you could go to a variety show 'without taking your pipe out of your mouth'. Smoking aside, it was all a question of money. Morgan couldn't lower his prices because of the 'steadily rising demand of the public for sumptuousness and elaboration in everything that relates to theatrical production'. Unfortunately, this could only be produced at prices that most of the Norwich population could not afford. Another great difficulty (the same one that every owner of the Theatre Royal has had to face since 1758) was the need to present a show that would fill both the pit and the gallery in addition to the circle and stalls. All managers had compromised catering 'for one class; and sometimes for another …The stalls people have seldom given me adequate support, except when a musical comedy has been running.' Morgan had been offered the chance of running a theatre in the north of England but had turned it down and was happy to stay in Norwich.

Morgan went to the magistrates and applied for his old license. Granting it to him, the Chairman of the Bench observed: 'You are returning to your old love, and we trust the public will support you thoroughly.' On 24 October 1904, the Theatre Royal was back in business with a full house. Making a break from the past year's variety shows, Morgan opened with a curtain-raiser, the farce *Aunt Rebecca* and followed it up with *Under Two Flags,* adapted from the popular novel by Ouida (Maria Louisa de la Ramee).

Under Two Flags

The play is an archetypical Foreign Legion story. The hero, Bertie Cecil, a young, handsome and popular aristocrat, has everything going for him but is bored by life. When he gets caught up in a gambling scandal, he decides to protect others involved by taking all the disgrace on himself and travelling to Algeria to join the *Chasseurs d'Afrique*. Over the coming 12 years he endures all kinds of hardship in the desert fighting but establishes himself as one of the *Chasseurs'* best soldiers. Then, the improbably-named Arab girl, Cigarette, who has fallen in love with him, manages to obtain the information he needs to clear his name from the scandal back in England. Bertie thus regains his title and marries the Princess Venetia Corona and lives happily ever after.

It was an undemanding play for sure, but a play nonetheless, and a major break from the ventriloquists and educated elephants of the previous year. The Norwich home of twice-nightly variety was now on the other side of the market place at the new Hippodrome in St Giles' Street.

It would be overstating things to say that the Theatre Royal catered for the high-brow residents of Norwich and the Hippodrome, the low-brow. Local people went to both establishments. And for several years the gallery crowd continued much the same at the Theatre Royal as a letter from 'disgusted' to the local paper in January 1905 made absolutely clear. 'Disgusted' complained that he had booked seats in the upper circle thinking he would be 'in the company of well-behaved people'. About ten minutes before the rise of the curtain, a group who had paid for gallery seats came and grabbed seats near him

> The conversation and language (not to mention the customary supply of nut shells and orange peeling) that was indulged in must have been very unpleasant to the women present.[116]

In 1913, Morgan began another major renovation of the theatre. He increased the size of the stage, making it 46 feet wide, 40 feet deep and 50 feet high and replaced the backless benches of the pit with proper stalls seats. But the renovations programme had to be called off in 1914 with the outbreak of the Great War. Morgan continued to put on a mixed programme of plays and musical comedies, but attendances dwindled during the war years.

The Maddermarket Theatre

One important event in Norwich theatre history that took place in the Bostock and Fitt years was the opening of Norwich's other well-known surviving theatre - the Maddermarket. The theatre was the creation of Nugent Monck, the founder of the amateur acting group The Norwich Players. Monck was committed to playing Shakespeare with the full text, in the Elizabethan style, and with simple scenery. In 1921, he purchased a one-time Catholic chapel built in the late 18th century and converted it into an Elizabethan playhouse. With its vaulted ceiling and galleries on three sides the theatre provided the ideal location for his Shakespearian (and other) productions.

The Theatre Royal after Fred Morgan's improvements

In December 1915, Morgan handed over the management of the theatre to Frank Rubens, who rebranded the theatre yet again, changing its title to the Empire and Theatre Royal and reverted back to twice-nightly variety shows. Rubens' tenure lasted only three months and, with Morgan's final retirement in March 1916, Bostock and Fitt regained control. They changed the name back again to the Theatre Royal and returned to a programme of plays that they ran as a complement to the variety shows playing at their other theatre, the Hippodrome. They continued in this way until March 1926, when they ceded control of the Theatre Royal to Jack Gladwin, who would remain in charge for the next three decades. The centenary of the new theatre building occurred during the short gap left between Bostock and Fitt's departure and Gladwin's arrival. It went uncelebrated.

Chapter 7

1926 - 1956: The Battle for Survival

In 1926, a decade after they had taken over the Theatre Royal, Bostock and Fitt had had enough. Once again it was rundown and in need of serious investment. Wanting to concentrate on their management of the Hippodrome and divest themselves of their interest in the older building, the partners approached another pair of established theatre managers, Jack Gladwin and Joe Collins, about taking over. Gladwin was the one they needed to persuade. Born not so far away in Lincolnshire, he had started his career as an actor round the turn of the century but had soon found his forte in theatre management. He began his managerial career as actor-manager of the Queen's Theatre in Swindon and had gone on to buy the theatre. One by one, he acquired interests in other theatres round the country. At the time he received Bostock and Fitt's invitation to buy the Theatre Royal, he was already in charge of Windsor's Theatre Royal, a theatre, similar

The theatre exterior that Gladwin found unattractive

to Norwich, dating back to Georgian times. He knew Norwich somewhat, having spent a week here in 1909 when his wife had played in a musical comedy, *A Trip to Chicago*, at the Theatre Royal.

He travelled up to Norwich with Collins on a cold winter's day to inspect the building. Their trip didn't start well. After having trouble finding the theatre, they were appalled at the dilapidated appearance of its exterior.

Gladwin later recalled on going inside it: 'We immediately sensed its atmosphere of great theatrical tradition.' Nonetheless, he and Collins decided they could do nothing with it. They stayed overnight in Norwich and arrived at the railway station the next morning to head for home but Bostock and Fitt were lying in wait for them in order to make one last pitch. Their ploy worked. Gladwin and Collins agreed there and then to lease the theatre for a year with an option to buy.

When they took over, they closed it for a month while carrying out some most pressing repairs. They then used their good connections to try and put together a varied programme of attractive shows at reasonable prices. They reopened with a musical revue entitled *Mr Tickle* starring the hugely-popular Scott and Whaley, a black-face act with humour derived from stereotypes of African Americans. Scott played the urban dandy with laughable pretensions to be treated like a white person and Whaley, with exaggerated painted lips, played the rural simpleton. When the box office opened the queues stretched along the street into Chapelfield. The second week the theatre staged one of Esmond's light-hearted romances, *Eliza Comes To Stay* - it proved just as successful. Gladwin and Collins soon decided to take up the option to buy and over the course of their first few months at the theatre, they invested in smartening it up, replacing the central heating, installing new lighting and putting in a new bar and foyer. Most importantly, they reinstated the tradition of the lavish Christmas pantomime that had faded out in the 1880s.

While the early prospects must have seemed quite rosy, Gladwin and Collins could not have realised the powerful competition that lay directly ahead. Radio and movies with sound were on the horizon.

Jack Gladwin, manager 1926-39, 1940-56

When radio programming began in 1922, very few homes had receivers. But this soon changed, as 'wireless' sets became cheaper and found their way into the homes of most of the local theatre-going public. Cinemas had been in Norwich almost 20 years before Gladwin's takeover, but there were limits to the competition that silent movies could provide. (Around this time, Norwich cinemas were often as noisy as the theatres with their lively piano accompaniment and the sounds of the literate reading out the captions to those who could not read.)[117] The first 'talkies' were shown in Norwich in 1928 just about the same time as radio receivers were being installed in Norwich homes. Bowing to these pressures in 1930, Bostock and Fitt abandoned live shows at the Hippodrome and switched to showing mainly films. This allowed the Theatre Royal to increase the number of variety and revue shows on its programme and strengthen the theatre's financial viability, if not its reputation, with local drama lovers and theatre critics.

Joe Collins died in 1931 and Gladwin acquired his part of the theatre equity. In comparison with the difficulties faced by many theatres in the country during the depressed years of the early 1930s, things were going reasonably well for the Theatre Royal. But a disaster that could well have closed the theatre forever was waiting.

The theatre burns down

On Friday, 22 June 1934, at about ten to two in the afternoon, the assistant cashier, Miss Bardwell, was sitting in the box office ready to sell tickets for the evening performance of a variety show with Alfredo and his Gypsy Orchestra topping the bill. (This was a popular act of the time, a group of gaily-costumed musicians performing songs such as *Lover Come Back Home* and *Come Play to Me Gypsy*.) She heard a clanging noise coming from the auditorium. Assuming it was Mr Leggat, the stage manager, she left the box office to see what he was doing. As she entered the auditorium, she smelt smoke and was horrified to see flames licking under the safety curtain. She rushed into the street to call for help. Coincidentally, George Smith, a night stagehand, was cycling past and already stopping to investigate. He and Miss Bardwell ran into the theatre where their worst suspicions were confirmed. Fire was burning underneath the stage on both sides of the safety curtain. The Fire Brigade was summonsed immediately. It was not far away and arrived quickly, but the situation was hopeless. A strong wind that day had intensified the flames and the speed with which they were spreading. According to the

local paper, 'a great crowd gathered and watched the melancholy spectacle of the rapid destruction of the theatre'. One person in the crowd was Geoffrey Watling, later the long-time chairman of Norwich City Football Club. He remembered the scene vividly:

> the police came along and kept us back ...we saw the flames. I remember it as if it was yesterday ...We were fascinated and very upset. Everybody was nearly in tears. We had not seen a fire like that in the city.[118]

Some sparks drifted over the then narrow Theatre Street to the Trinity Presbyterian Church, setting its roof on fire. The Fire Brigade extinguished these flames but could do nothing for the theatre building.

Fighting the flames

The fire destroyed not only the building but also many irreplaceable souvenirs of the theatre's history such as old playbills and framed pictures of the great performers who had trodden its boards. Alfredo and members of his orchestra lost much in the fire. They had been rehearsing on stage the morning of the fire and had left some of their instruments and musical arrangements behind. They were all destroyed. In a stroke of great fortune, however, the piano arrangements, charred at the edges but otherwise legible, were found in the debris. Their costumes were also rescued unscathed and the next evening the company performed two shows at St Andrew's Hall with instruments loaned to them by members of the Norwich City Municipal Orchestra.

After the fire, June 1934

Frank Crane, a stagehand at the time, recalled how he was in Chapelfield when he saw the smoke.[119] He raced back and watched attempts to save the carpet in the foyer. It was a massive carpet and was soaking wet from the firemen's hoses. It took 14 men to roll it up and to lift it out to safety into Lady Lane just across from the theatre. According to Frank, when they went back later, they couldn't find it. The mystery of where it went puzzled theatre workers over the following years.

Gladwin was at his home in Brighton on the day of the fire and as soon as he heard the news he came up to Norwich. On the journey, did he feel any temptation to pocket the insurance money and call it a day? Apparently not. He later said that he

> determined in the train that I would build a new up-to-date theatre on the same site and none other. Nothing but my deep sentiment for the great traditions of the theatre in Norwich would have induced me to make such a decision.[120]

It is unlikely that it was only these sentiments that made him rebuild. He must have also felt that theatre audiences in the Norwich area were big enough to make the new building a viable concern. Indeed, on another occasion, he said that he would not have erected such a large new building without the 'faith that a large section of the citizens still have a real appreciation of the art of the theatre'.

The third Theatre Royal building

On arrival, Gladwin looked over the ruined building and announced his intention to have the theatre rebuilt and ready for the Christmas pantomime. This was over-optimistic, but it was completed in just over a year, largely because he used a standard off-the-peg design that was being used for the Odeon cinemas that were then being built round the country. The total cost came to about £75,000 (about £3.5 million in 2007 terms).

The demolition begins

Several commentators since have questioned whether, if Gladwin had spent a bit longer planning, some of the design problems that subsequent managers have had to deal with could have been avoided. One writer in a technical theatre journal commented:

> It seems strange, in the light of modern thinking, that a theatre could have been so badly designed. It was not on a very large site but this was no excuse for the inside. The foyer and entrances seemed to have been designed to make it as difficult as possible to get into the auditorium. The sight lines were not good in the stalls, the stage was raked, had little wing space, no storage whatsoever … the dressing rooms were few, small and cold.[121]

But that was written in 1971. On its opening in 1935, it was hailed as one of the most modern in design and best-equipped theatres in the country. It was certainly a great improvement on the 1826-built theatre it had replaced. It had the structure it has today with 1500 seats on two levels. Audience comfort and ease of access to the auditorium was much better than before. Even more significant were the changes on the other side of the curtain. The new stage was much better equipped and made possible more technically-demanding productions. The exterior was designed in a contemporary art-deco design and finished in white tiles. These became unpopular later as fashions changed and were sometimes referred to as 'white lavatory tiles'.

The new theatre opened on 30 September 1935 with the Lord Mayor, Mr P. W. Jewson, joining the audience in a production of *White Horse Inn,* an immensely-popular musical that had opened in the West End in 1931. Performed by a large company from the London Coliseum, the action took place in an Austrian inn in a stereotypical idyllic alpine setting. With the obligatory happy ending, it provided an ideal route to escape the, sometimes, harsh realities of 1930s Britain. The production exploited the possibilities of the new stage by setting the scenery on a revolving platform, which impressed the audiences. The play was performed by one of the touring companies of the impresario Prince Littler, who later managed the Theatre Royal for a season. The theatre

The new Theatre Royal with its white tile exterior

carried on where it had left off with a varied programme of entertainment. Gladwin managed to bring in some big names contracting Sybil Thorndike in 1936 to appear with her husband, Lewis Casson, in *Six Men of Dorset*.

During the late-1930s, the period of increasing competition from the movies reached its zenith as new cinemas sprouted up in the suburbs. In 1938, two new cinemas opened in Norwich: the Regal on Dereham Road and the Ritz on Larkman Lane. In 1939, Gladwin required a serious operation. In the face of his own uncertain future, with increased competition from the cinemas and with the prospects of war looming, he seemed to lose the resolve to carry on. He said that after 40 years in the theatrical business (and considering his present age) he should take things a little bit easier. So he agreed to lease the Theatre Royal to Prince Littler for 21 years. Reassuring Norwich theatregoers, Gladwin promised that Littler would be the 'ideal man to maintain the reputation of the theatre'.

Littler was still under the age of 40 but had already managed six other theatres and continued to run half-a-dozen touring companies each year. He said all the right things - how he appreciated 'the long and rich dramatic history associated with the theatre in Norwich' and how he would aim not only to uphold its prestige, but also 'try and advance it in accord with modern standards'. He claimed he would rather make a little out of good shows than a lot from inferior ones and boasted that he was in a better position to provide important and big attractions at the Theatre Royal than Gladwin because he could, with his circuit of theatres, 'offer great inducement to prominent companies to come here'.[122] The magistrates transferred the theatre license to him on 3 April 1939. Littler reduced prices for his twice-nightly shows to bring them in line with cinema prices but in the end he found it difficult to make a go of it. After one difficult season, facing all the constraints imposed by the Second World War that began in the September, he found that Norwich's 'long and rich dramatic history' was not enough to hold him. By this time, however, Jack Gladwin had recovered unexpectedly well from his operation and his doctor had given him the all-clear to resume work and, he was pleased to report, 'to indulge once again in a good cigar'. He willingly took back the lease from Prince Littler and told the local paper that he was more attached to Norwich's Theatre Royal than any of his other theatres:

> I have said before, and I repeat it now, that I have a genuine sentimental attachment to the Theatre Royal. I loved the old building and its notable associations with the dramatic history of this country.[123]

On 26 April 1940, just one year after his withdrawal, Gladwin was back in charge. He was an unassuming and shy man who would not have been recognised by most of his patrons, but he loved the manager's job. Asked once about his reluctance to make public appearances, he said 'it is all very well to be in the limelight on the stage, but I don't like it elsewhere'.[124]

The Second World War years

Things went quite well for the Theatre Royal during the war years. Apart from a three-week break in September when hostilities commenced, the theatre remained open throughout. In the early days of the war when the air-raid sirens were sounded, the lights went up and the manager came on stage to tell the audience. Later, signs were placed on each side of the stage and lit up when the sirens sounded. The warnings gave those in the audience who wanted to time to seek shelter in the near-by Chapelfield bomb shelter. There were no enemy-action casualties at the theatre, although Gladwin did have a narrow escape at a cinema near his Sussex home. He was watching a film when the theatre took a direct hit. Some members of the audience were killed, but he survived with a shrapnel injury to a finger.

Many buildings in the city centre were destroyed by bombs during the war but the Theatre Royal managed to escape, although not without some close shaves. The theatre management employed two or three men to stay in the building through the night on fire-watch. Maurice King, a stagehand at the time, recalled how, when they were on watch, they used the under-stage space as their bomb shelter. He remembered snatching some sleep on the grand piano covered by a couple of drapes. One night, he was on duty with Frank Crane and Stanley Fuller (who later became the theatre's long-serving house manager). He had gone to make himself a cup of tea when he heard Fuller shouting:

'Quick the theatre's on fire.' We rushed out into the auditorium and it was full of white smoke. We then started to search the building to find out where the fire was. We all kept together. We went up the steps to the balcony and there on the stone steps, through the smoke, we saw two firebombs. One at the top and one near the bottom. They were not much more than a foot long. They were still smoking but the flames had gone. We went down to the auditorium again and saw a brown patch on the ceiling. One of the bombs had got in the false roof. We took a panel off the air duct near the ceiling and Frank and I crawled through it to another panel. We took that off and squeezed through into the false roof where there was a light. There was the firebomb. It had come through the roof and had landed on the wire netting upper layer of the plaster ceiling. By then, like the other two, it had burned out and there was no damage caused other than a big scorched patch on the ceiling. If it had gone through the ceiling and landed in the auditorium, it would have burned the theatre down and I might not be here to tell the tale now.[125]

In 1940, the theatre survived a much bigger bomb that fell in Theatre Street but failed to explode.

George Swain's picture of the removal of the Theatre Street bomb. Lieutenant Hanby (chief of the Bomb Disposal Unit) is listening with his stethoscope applied to the fuse. Given the proximity allowed to the photographer and the nonchalance of the men, it is most probable that the bomb had already been made safe.

During the war years, when theatres in London were closed, Gladwin did rather better in attracting established stars such as Donald Wolfit and Evelyn Laye to come to Norwich. The Theatre Royal continued to run a programme with a good mix of plays, musicals and variety shows. On the other side of the market place, the Hippodrome (no longer a cinema) presented mainly variety revues, the titles of which point to efforts to attract the growing number of single servicemen in the camps and bases dotted round the city. Titles of revues for the summer of 1940 included:

Nuit des Femmes

Follow the Girls

Strip Please

Don't Be Shy

Don't Blush Girls

Naughty But Nice

The revues were often quite edgy. On 26 April 1940, Hylda Baker (She knows you know!) and five others were convicted for using material not approved by the Lord Chamberlain. The Norwich Watch Committee had a reputation for being particularly tough. The Theatre Royal shows were more decorous but on the week beginning 9 September 1940 it did make something of a counter-attack by presenting *The Bare Idea* - 'a screamingly funny farcical comedy about a nudist colony'. It also included nude *tableaux vivants* in some of its variety productions.

Towards the end of the war, the Theatre Royal was licensed to put on shows on Sundays 'solely for members of the forces' as long as no admission was charged and as long as every man and woman in attendance was in uniform. These shows were a great success and attracted packed houses every week.

Maurice King's memories

Maurice King, the stagehand who found the firebombs in the theatre, has many vivid memories of the wartime years that give an insightful feel into the Theatre Royal experience of those days.[126]

The tableaux vivants

I remember in one variety show there was a striptease artist called Phyllis Dixey. She used to do these poses. She couldn't move. In those days you couldn't if you were a nude. Well, they wanted someone to pull the curtains. And I said, 'Yeah, I'll do that for a pound a week.' (I'd have given them a pound a week!) Phyllis used to come on stage behind closed curtains in a dressing gown which she would take off and hide behind the scenery. She would be in the all-together apart from what looked like a big piece of sticking plaster to hide one part of her body. She also used to have a loose piece of chiffon that she draped in different ways for each pose. Phyllis would then strike a pose on the sofa or the chair (it was a very simple set) and then nod at me to open the curtains. After a while, I'd pull the curtains shut and she'd get into another pose. She'd then nod at me to open the curtains again.

Phyllis Dixey was at the height of her fame in the 1940s. She began her show-business career singing and reciting in variety shows and at the beginning of the War joined up with ENSA (Entertainments National Service Association). In her concerts for the troops, she said that she felt she could do most to help the brave boys by letting them see her posed artistically and without clothes on the stage. Since nudity was only permitted if the performer remained perfectly immobile, her first performances were in tableaux vivants of the kind Maurice describes. However, in 1942, she recruited a company of girls and mounted a show called the *Whitehall Follies* in which the performers danced fan-and-feather dances and moved around as they took of their clothes. This revue at the Whitehall Theatre in London was the West End's first genuine striptease show. Phyllis stayed on at the theatre producing her *Peek-a-Boo* revues until 1947 and was widely known as the 'Queen of Striptease. She always considered her shows to be works of art and absolutely respectable. She was appalled by the more explicit shows that opened in Soho and refused to change her style. She died forgotten, aged 50 in 1964.

The circuses

The circus was sold out. There were ever so many people outside. You've never seen any-thing like it. The police were called and everything. So we stage workers had to go and double up with people on the door, trying to keep the crowds out. We never collected tickets or anything. Well, we couldn't. It was Bedlam. There were so many kids that had never seen a circus before and they were desperate. We couldn't stop them, so we just let everybody in and that was that. They were sitting down in the aisles and everywhere.

They were particularly waiting to see the elephants that had walked to the theatre from the railway station up Prince of Wales Road in one long line holding each others' tails. The stage manager told me that the elephants knew whether the stage would be strong enough to hold them. The first one would put his foot on the stage and test it. If he felt it was unsafe, he would turn around and come back, and none of the other elephants would go on. If he kept going on to the stage, the rest would happily follow him. The night they first went on, I went underneath the stage when they were dancing and saw that all the girders were going up and down. I ran up and told Frank. 'Strike a light,' he said looking frightened. He quickly got a four-by-four plank and we wedged it under the stage. And then, just as we relaxed a bit, an elephant did a wee. It poured through the stage and went all over Frank. What a horrible smell! No one would go anywhere near him for a week.

At another circus, there was an act by Tony Kay, performed in the smallest lion cage in the world. It was only about five-foot square. Every night he would enter the cramped cage and make the lion beg, roll over, roar and look angry and do the usual tricks. The audience used to think he was in great danger. But we knew differently; Leo was a very old lion with no teeth. When Tony Kay came out of the cage he'd be really hot and sweaty and would go back to his dressing room to cool off. When the show had finished, we had to hang around and wait for ages for him to return and supervise Leo's transfer from the small cage to his larger travelling cage. Well, one night, we got fed up and thought we'd do it ourselves. So we linked the small cage to the bigger one and prodded Leo to walk up the ramp between them. When the lion tamer arrived, he went ballistic: 'Whatever would you have you done if the lion had got out?' I replied: 'Well he wouldn't hurt you in any case.' 'Well that's not the point', the lion tamer said warning us never to do it again.

Maurice King (third from left) with theatre staff in 1940

The conjurer's stooge

I worked as a stooge for a conjurer, the Great Murray, in a variety show. I had to put on a coat with several rabbits squirming in different pockets and then sit out in the auditorium. Murray chose me every night as the 'randomly picked member of the audience'. I'd go on stage, pretend to be amazed as the rabbits were pulled out and then go back and sit in the audience. I'd chat to my neighbours for a while, and then, as soon as I could without raising suspicion, return backstage. All these extra jobs were paid an extra 12s. 6d. or even £1 a week on top of regular wages and were quite sought after.

The ice shows

I didn't look forward to ice shows. We had to put tubes on the stage, pour on water and then turn on the engine that would freeze it. On the Saturday night we turned the engine off. That meant it became a bit dodgy for the skaters on the last performance as the ice was starting to melt. On the Sunday morning, we all used to go back to the theatre to get rid of the ice, so the next week's show could be set up in time. They'd give us a pickaxe to break up the ice. We'd then pick up lumps of it and throw it on a lorry outside. You can imagine, by the time we finished, we were soaked. It was terrible.

The failure of live theatre as the 200th anniversary approaches

With the dawn of the 1950s, it again became increasingly difficult to run theatres at a profit. Many provincial theatres closed their doors. This contraction in theatrical venues and in audiences led to a contraction in the number of high-quality touring companies. By August 1956, Gladwin was 81 years old and losing the energy needed to keep fighting. So, when his doctor ordered him to rest, he persuaded two good friends - L. Kemp and J. Will Collins - to lease the theatre from him. He told the local paper: 'I have not felt lately that I have had the energy to devote to the business of bookings that I should have done. It is almost impossible today to get sufficient attractions of a good standard.' He hoped that Kemp and Collins had the experience necessary for success. Kemp was chairman and managing director of Eastern Counties Cinemas Ltd. and had supervised the construction of many cinemas while Collins (incidentally, the father of Joan and Jackie Collins) operated the Will Collins Theatrical & Vaudeville Exchange Ltd. and Queensway Productions Ltd. He had experience in theatre management including the booking of shows. The two entrepreneurs started off optimistically with plans to turn the theatre's finances round by including movies in the mix of plays, musicals and variety. To pacify critics who wanted to maintain a year-round programme of live performances, they promised that only 'outstanding' films would be shown and, to demonstrate that the Theatre Royal would remain a cut above the Hippodrome, they declared that the stage shows 'would not include nudes'. They also promised to spend £10,000 on improvements especially to the entrance and exit to the circle. Gladwin told those who objected to the new direction the theatre was taking that, had he stayed, he would have had to do the same and supplement plays with cinema and variety performances. He said he would keep his London office open and would continue to try to secure good shows for the Theatre Royal.

After a few weeks - and having lost money on some touring plays - Kemp and Collins reverted back to twice-nightly variety and toned down their hopes for financial success. On 8 December 1956, the press announced that Kemp and Collins had given up and that Gladwin had leased the theatre to Essoldo, the UK's third largest cinema chain. Norwich theatre enthusiasts were devastated at what seemed the end of the road for a theatre only a few months shy of its 200th anniversary. Perhaps the spirits of the great early performers were offended at the prospect of the theatre becoming a cinema. During the Christmas pantomime that opened that month, there were three serious accidents: the wardrobe mistress incurred a very deep cut in her thumb; Angela Kinman, the principal girl, slipped on stage and cut her wrist on some scenery. Bleeding profusely for the rest of the scene she had six stitches during a costume change but did not miss an entrance. Miss Reno, one of the artistes in a trapeze segment of the pantomime, was less fortunate. She missed her grip, flew at speed into the curtain and dropped 14 feet to the stage. Her trajectory into the curtain was fortuitous; if she had gone into the wall the consequences would have been much more serious. As it was, she was not fit enough to return to the stage before the pantomime closed.

Gladwin retired to his golf. If he felt any remorse for his decision to lease and eventually sell the Theatre Royal to a cinema chain, he had the satisfaction to live on just long enough to see the theatre restored to its original role. He died in 1969 at the age of 94.

Chapter 8

1956 - 1992: The Theatre Royal Reborn

The Theatre Royal becomes an Essoldo cinema

When Essoldo took over the Theatre Royal in 1956, it presented a year-round programme of films, interrupted only by occasional weekend concerts, the Christmas pantomime and a few other special events. Those who hoped that the theatre would at least be a higher-class cinema were soon disappointed. Essoldo gave the Theatre Royal no special treatment and like other cinemas on their circuit, it screened films most likely to make the most profit. In its first year of operation there were several letters to the local press complaining about the low standard of the films, particularly X-certificated films. Ernest Wells, the manager, riposted:

> The correspondence condemning cinemas for showing films which are plainly of only box-office value, as against cultural value, is also quite ridiculous. What do people imagine we are in business for?[127]

On 21 June 1959, on the site where Edmund Kean, Mrs Sarah Siddons and other theatre immortals had played, the Theatre Royal ran a 'Nell Gwynne Sex Kitten Contest' with a film contract as the first prize.

Essoldo did not invest in the building. In 1960, there were several complaints about how rundown it had become with its ripped seats and torn-out ashtrays. Partly because of its poor reputation, it proved difficult to bring back the old regulars even when the theatre staged serious plays. In October 1962, Essoldo presented a live production of *Billy Liar,* a play that had enjoyed a long West End run with Albert Finney in the lead role. The house was almost empty on opening night and even at the final performance there were only about 250 in the audience. The long-serving house manager, Stanley Fuller, said: 'What puzzles me is that, after all the talk about the need for a live theatre in the city, when you get a first-class play, people do not come.'[128]

In the mid-1960s, many theatres and cinemas were being profitably transformed into high-prize bingo halls. Essoldo sought planning permission in 1965 to make a similar conversion of the Theatre Royal. Several months later, with the application pending, the company announced that it would not renew its live theatre license. After more than

200 years, the Theatre Royal was facing a death sentence. This spurred Norwich City Council into action.

To understand the council's intervention, two contemporary background issues need to be taken into account: the fate of the Norwich Hippodrome and the debate about the building of a new Norwich Civic Theatre.

The demise of the Hippodrome

Soon after the Theatre Royal had converted to a cinema, the Hippodrome broke away from its recent tradition of presenting variety and films and converted itself into the Norfolk Playhouse, the home of a repertory company of professional actors under the direction of Hector Ross and his actress wife, June Sylvaine.[129] It got off to a good start with a production of Noel Coward's latest play, *South Sea Bubble*. However, despite high-quality productions by the company, the venture lasted little more than a year, seemingly proving once and for all that it was impossible to make a profit in Norwich by producing just plays. The local press first reported the theatre's closure in early March 1959. Once again, keen theatrelovers were appalled, but one correspondent to the local newspaper advised people to face up to the inevitable:

> Do not throw blame upon the public for enjoying the type of entertainment that is convenient; if the live theatre cannot compete then it must unfortunately and inevitably close. This is the end of an era, the end of families trooping religiously to the cinema week after week, the end of live theatre, which, although pleasantly enjoyed in the past, is now on the threshold of a serious and inevitable decline.[130]

Ernest Wells, the Theatre Royal's manager, obviously agreed with this statement. Four days later, he wrote that

The demolition of the Hippodrome in 1966

no live performances, not even musicals, were financially viable in Norwich. Touring musical shows had become too expensive to bring in without a subsidy. The city had earned itself a reputation as a theatrical graveyard and it was, in any case, difficult to persuade performers to come.

The repertory company at the Hippodrome regrouped in April for one final attempt to make a go of it but to no avail. The theatre closed on 20 June 1959. That same week six other resident companies in Britain had to disband as well. The Hippodrome reopened shortly after as a cinema but closed for good on 27 April 1960. The losses had been of such a magnitude (takings on the final day amounted to only £3) that the owner was forced to declare bankruptcy. It became the sixth cinema to close in Norwich in four years.

In May 1960, the press reported that there were proposals to demolish the theatre and that the council would not step in to save the building. The report triggered a number of petitions to save the Hippodrome, but they failed and the theatre was sold for development in June 1960. The building changed hands a number of times over the coming few years and was finally purchased by the council itself in 1966. It was then demolished to make way for the St Giles' Street multi-storey car park. This development, which angered some of the electorate, occurred just a few months before the council had to decide the fate of the city's other major theatre, the Theatre Royal.

Plans for a new civic theatre

Some three years after the closure and sale of the Hippodrome, Norwich City Council set up a working party to consider the establishment of a new type of professional theatre in the city. In July 1964, the council approved the idea of erecting a new theatre as part of a renewed civic centre. David Percival, the city architect, presented plans for a relatively-small octagonal building that could be used for 'theatre-in-the-round' productions. Several councillors had misgivings with some suggesting that the money would be better allocated towards the cost of building a multi-purpose assembly hall at the University of East Anglia on the outskirts of the city. Finally, in November 1965, the council met to decide whether to give the go-ahead for the construction of a new civic theatre with 590 seats at a cost of £306,000. The critics complained that in difficult economic times the theatre would be a 'charming luxury', an unneeded 'status symbol'. Over their objections, the construction was approved, albeit only 'when funds [were] available'. It was this clause, that would ultimately save the Theatre Royal.

In January 1966, when the long-closed Hippodrome building was put up for sale by its latest owners, some people called for Norwich City Council to buy it and to convert it into the civic theatre, thereby saving the costs associated with building something brand new. The city did buy the building but, as already noted, did not transform it into a civic theatre but into a car park.

The Theatre Royal becomes the civic theatre

In November 1965, the Essoldo Group placed an application before Norwich City Council asking for change of use for the Theatre Royal so it could be used for bingo games. The city council obviously did not like the idea but in turning it down could only give reasons that the Essoldo felt optimistic it could get reversed on appeal, namely that:

- Advertising signs would be detrimental to the area.

- More traffic would be generated during the day.

- Bingo was an inappropriate activity in the heart of the civic centre.

Soon after the rejection, the Essoldo Group exercised a clause in its lease and purchased the Theatre Royal building for £50,000 and then, in September 1966, appealed against the refusal to the Minister of Housing and Local Government. Essoldo repudiated the council's claims and stressed that it would make no major structural alterations to the building, which could still be used for live shows. At the hearing in October, it told the inquiry that the Theatre Royal could not continue operating profitably as a theatre or as a cinema. Even the latest pantomime (usually one of the season's most profitable productions) had made a loss. Perhaps to prove a point, a series of plays were presented in the autumn and, as predicted, they made a loss - £800 in the first two weeks of November.[131] About this time, those who had suggested the council buy the Hippodrome for the civic theatre suggested it purchase the Theatre Royal instead.

Things dragged on inconclusively for the next few weeks until March 1967 when the Essoldo Group announced it did not plan to renew its license for live performances at the Theatre Royal. As the *Eastern Evening News* headline announced, the city faced a 'Theatre Crisis'. Conscious that this notion of a theatre crisis had taken hold in the electorate - and perhaps not confident of winning the appeal - the city council decided to negotiate to buy the building. The sale was made the following month and the building changed hands for £90,000 (over £1 million in 2007 prices). In announcing the purchase, the council declared that the Theatre Royal would now become the civic theatre. It also declared that it intended to spend a further £300,000 (part of which would come from a hopefully substantial grant from the Arts Council of Great Britain) to improve the stage and to convert the theatre building into a multi-purpose centre that would include a restaurant and an exhibition space. David Percival, the city architect - who had been influenced by the new Abbey Theatre that had opened in Dublin in 1966 - explained plans to make the auditorium size adjustable by creating a movable partition behind the first six rows of the circle. This would allow for a variable seating capacity between 730 and 1350. The smaller space would be suitable for most plays and the larger space for operas and other such events likely to attract good-size audiences. The building, therefore, would be much more versatile than the planned new civic theatre that would now not be constructed. Moreover, renovating the Theatre Royal in this way would prove cheaper (at least on a per-seat basis) than a newly-built civic centre. With the sale completed, Essoldo's planning appeal was allowed to lapse.

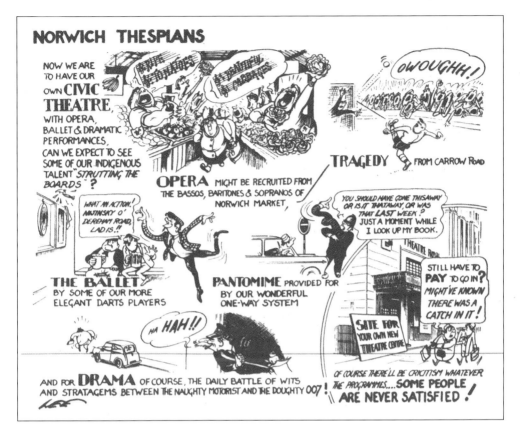

Following this announcement, a heated debate was played out both in the local press and on the doorsteps during the May local election campaign. Most theatregoers applauded the council's decision, although some regretted that the Hippodrome, with its superior acoustics, had been overlooked. Those opposed to investment in a civic theatre were the most vociferous. They railed against Arthur South, the Labour leader of Norwich City Council, for using ratepayers' money for this 'wanton extravagance'. One writer to the local paper reminded conscience-stricken backers of the Theatre Royal of the appalling support they had given the theatre over the years and urged them to:

> put their pens away and let the poor old place die peacefully…The sooner the people of Norwich realise that they relinquished all rights to a theatre many years ago, then the better it will be.

The council mandated a group of local government officers to put the theatre into a holding operation by planning a mix of films and shows. However, things started badly. They booked a big production of the successful West End musical, *Robert and Elizabeth*, in October 1967. It cost a total of £7273 to stage but drew only £3902 in receipts. A season of plays followed produced by Zak Matalon (husband of actress Elisabeth Seal) but it attracted very small audiences. There were calls to pull the plug before more ratepayers' money was poured down the drain. Opposition grew stronger in December when it was announced that the cost of renovating the theatre might top £500,000 (more

Controversy, pathos, suspense – what a fascinating play it would make

than £6 million in 2007 terms). It grew stronger and later in the year, when indications of the operating deficit were becoming clearer, it was estimated that financing the theatre could add one-and-a-half pence to the rates. In April 1968, Conservative councillors put their weight behind calls for the theatre to be regionally financed and for Norwich City Council not to foot the £500,000 bill alone. A cartoon in the *Eastern Evening News* summed up the situation well. A performer is sitting in a dressing-room reading about the ongoing local debate: 'controversy, pathos, suspense - what a fascinating play it would make!'

Fortunately, by this time, the theatre was going much better under the professional guidance of Laurence Hill, a man whose life had been spent in show-business. He had started off in the cinema and at the age of 18 became the Gaumont chain's youngest chief projectionist. During the Second World War he was employed in organising drama and entertainment for the troops and on demobilisation joined his relatives, George and Alfred Black, as a theatre impresario. His health broke down in 1961 and he retired to Norfolk to recover and escape the stresses of the London theatre world. Six years later, seeing the theatrical developments on his doorstep and feeling in better health, he volunteered his services to the Theatre Royal and worked energetically using his rich source of contacts in the entertainment industry. He put together an attractive programme and slashed ticket prices to attract in new customers. One of his first great successes was the presentation of the Osipov Balalaika Orchestra from Moscow. The show took receipts of over £21,000 in a fortnight. In May 1968, he persuaded stars from the Bolshoi Ballet to perform in Norwich and sold 20,000 seats, enough to balance the books. The Soviet Ambassador attended one of the performances and the resulting publicity put the Norwich Theatre Royal back on the theatrical map. The success of the ballet carried over and the play, *Not Now Darlings,* starring Donald Sinden and Bernard Cribbins, followed on its pre-London opening tour. It sold 9000 seats or about 75 per cent of capacity. Receipts for this play were the highest in the theatre's history. By June, Hill had managed to turn the theatre's finances round and plays thereafter regularly showed a modest profit.

By the summer of 1968, people were questioning the necessity of partitioning the theatre to decrease the size of the auditorium for plays. At the end of the summer, this plan was dropped from active consideration as, too, were plans for creating a Norwich professional repertory company for the Theatre Royal. The Theatre Royal would continue with a variety of touring shows. Some people, particularly Andrew Ryrie, chairman of the Theatre Working Party, reacted with fierce disappointment to the news.[132] In November 1969, all of the original civic theatre plans were dropped and a more modest renovation plan calling for an outlay of only £128,000 (with £68,000 coming from the Arts Council) was put forward to the council. It was also proposed that while the council would own the building, the administration would be placed in the hands of a theatre trust. The council would rent the theatre to the trust at a peppercorn rent and - for a period of five years - guarantee to cover a deficit of £15,000 to £20,000. (Since the takeover, the theatre had been running at an annual deficit of about £16,000.) The following month the plan was approved, but not without a fight. One opponent complained that the Norwich public had been conned into corporate ownership of the theatre. As the *Evening News* reported, there was a 'vociferous section of public opinion' that was strongly against 'having a theatre on the rates'.[133]

During the summer of 1968, Parliament repealed the 1843 Theatres Act and replaced it with a new law abolishing the censorship powers of the Lord Chamberlain. The new law allowed performances of sex comedies that were popular with Norwich audiences for a period during the 1970s. Local opposition was not strong enough to halt the performance of these plays but it was strong enough (in 1968) to halt the Soviet Red Army Ensemble. Following the great success of the Bolshoi Ballet, the Red Army Ensemble had been booked for September, but the invitation had to be rescinded in the face of protests about the recent Soviet invasion of Czechoslovakia.

The renovations finally took place in 1970. While the building was certainly made more comfortable for audiences, the biggest changes undertaken were behind the curtain, where the raked stage was levelled and the dressing rooms - those 'cramped corridors of cells' - enlarged and made more comfortable. The unpopular 'lavatory-tile' look of the façade was replaced but only by a 'severe but imposing frontage of brick and steel cladding'. The theatre reopened in December with a gala performance of *The Nutcracker* by the London Festival Ballet. The performance was preceded by a prologue written for the occasion by Christopher Fry.

One change after the reopening that greatly increased the comfort of most of the spectators was the removal of all the ashtrays and a ban on smoking. There were a few patrons who vigorously objected to this, one of whom wrote to the local paper:

> Having arrived at the theatre recently with my wife and four friends for an enjoyable evening, I found to my surprise that there is now a smoking ban, so instead of having an enjoyable evening, my friends and I had a fairly miserable one as we all enjoy a smoke during the show.[134]

He suggested that since local smokers had helped finance the theatre it would only be fair if smoking were permitted on alternate nights. The debate in the correspondence columns ran for a few days. The paper itself ran a straw poll on the issue and reported its results: 'Unanimous! Keep That Ban on Smoking.'[135]

Hill's success led the Arts Council in March 1970 to designate the Theatre Royal as one of 12 large theatres on its 'national touring grid'. Hill stayed at the helm after the 1970 renovations for a further year before ill health once again pushed him into retirement. He had achieved a great deal. By the time he left, annual subsidies had been secured from Norfolk County Council and Norwich City Council as well as Arts Council transport subsidies that brought in coachloads of patrons from as far as 70 miles away.

The Dick Condon years

Dick Condon at the time of his appointment

With Hill's resignation, adverts were placed for a new general manager at a salary of £3000 to £3500 per year. From a pool of 65 applicants, Richard Condon was given the job. It's unlikely that anyone on the interviewing panel realised how controversial the soft-spoken and likeable Irishman would prove, how quickly he would bring the theatre into profitability or how he would make the Theatre Royal one of the most talked-about theatres in the country; in short, how he would turn out to be what a later *TV Times* blurb termed a 'theatrical atom bomb'.[136]   The first surprise Condon sprung was declining the appointment committee's offer of a guaranteed salary of over £3000 a year. He said he would take only £1750 but with a bonus equivalent to 1 per cent of the profits when the turnover exceeded £100,000 a year. (He reached that goal in just six months.)

At the time of his appointment in July 1972, Condon was 34 years old. He recalled that when he replied to the advertisement he hadn't even known where Norwich was. And, just like Gladwin and Collins before him, he claimed that after arriving in the city he had trouble finding the theatre. Condon had been associated with the stage since he was 14 both as an actor and as an administrator. He had US citizenship (which he gained through his father) but had grown up poor in Ireland. There, as a youth, he had been thrilled by show business and had 'mitched' potatoes to sell to get money to go the circus. A consummate salesman, he liked to tell the story of how he had set off for a visit to the United States with a case full of cheaply-produced sew-on Irish Emblems and had sold them for a profit of $17,000. Back in Ireland, he had argued his way into acting jobs and later moved into theatre management. He was the general manager of the Olympia Theatre in Dublin for most of the 1960s and, when it closed, he put together the finance to buy it and reopen it. In his first year, he registered a comfortable profit. From 1963 onwards, he also worked as administrator of the Dublin Theatre Festival. His considerable success in that city made his application for the job in Norwich stand out. Condon, self-confessedly, conformed to all but one of the stereotypes of the stage Irishman. He was a drinker, a gambler and a believing Catholic, particularly after his successful recovery from throat cancer at the age of 28. (He once told Joan Bakewell that, in his car, he never stopped speaking to God.)[137] Above anything else he had the gift of the blarney and later became known for persuading companies to come to the Theatre Royal for much less than their original asking prices. (One person who had dealt with Condon claimed: 'He didn't kiss that blarney stone, he swallowed the bloody thing.') Where he did not conform to a stereotype was in his appetite for work. He was a self-confessed workaholic who attacked his job with enormous energy, spending almost all of his waking hours, from early morning and often until midnight or later, at the theatre. He claimed that he never took a holiday. He spent most of his life providing leisure for other people but said 'I can't stand it myself'. He admitted that he consciously played out the stage Irishman role. 'A stage Irishman', he once said, 'can get away with anything.'[138]

Condon playing the Irishman with house manager Stanley Fuller and technical director Jack Bowhill

The unusual contract he signed demonstrated Condon's commitment to making the theatre profitable and profitability in his eyes could only be achieved by bringing non-traditional patrons into the theatre. This meant targeting more and more people in an expanded advertising campaign and also broadening the programme to appeal to a wider spectrum of the population. Condon felt that advertising had hitherto been sporadic and inconsistent, 'part of a cunning plot to defy people to find out what was on, in case they might come'.[139] He quadrupled the advertising budget and made sure that both the local population and the theatre industry knew that an exciting new era had begun. Fluorescent banners were mounted outside the theatre and new montages of photographs and posters inside. Full-colour advertisements were placed in the local papers. (He later admitted that he had set out to give the advertising a 'circus-like gaudiness'.) Milkmen distributed leaflets on their rounds, agents sold tickets in outlying villages and special rail/theatre packages were put together. Condon even instituted a Theatre Royal savings stamps scheme. He went on radio telling listeners that the theatre was their theatre and imploring them to 'Come as you are, in overalls if you have no time to change, but come.' In his early days, he even went out on to the streets to buttonhole passers-by and urge them to buy tickets. He often greeted people as they arrived for evening performances and would drink with them in the bar afterwards. One person commented that it was always worthwhile going to the Theatre Royal because even if the play was dull Dick Condon would always be amusing in the bar after the show.[140] Condon wanted to transform the theatre into a brash and welcoming place and not 'a mausoleum where you had to tiptoe in to find a seat'. He made sure that this was known across the country and placed advertisements proclaiming the theatre's success in the trade press. In April 1973 a box advert in *The Stage*, told theatre actors and administrators that the Theatre Royal was the place to come to.

Attendance at the theatre increased and the books moved into the black. However, many traditional

THEATRE ROYAL
NORWICH
Currently smashing all old box office records
Going live for the entire season 1973
General Manager: Dick Condon
Telephone: Norwich 60955
The liveliest entertainment centre
in Britain's Eastern Region

theatregoers were uneasy at what was going on. Those who had hoped for a civic theatre to provide a programme of intellectually-stimulating plays and music and other 'high-culture' events were appalled. Condon took these critics on pugnaciously and without compromise. As he said in an interview:

> For anything I believe in, I will go through fire and water … I don't believe in compromise … compromise leads to a lukewarm mid-stream and always ends in mediocrity.[141]

A good example of this aggressive outlook was his extraordinary exchange with the respected historian, Corelli Barnett. In November 1972, Barnett wrote a letter to the *Eastern Daily Press* complaining how Condon was 'spoiling the simple and sophisticated elegance' of the Theatre Royal by introducing crudely-coloured banners, coloured light bulbs, canned music and small plastic refuse bags along the seat backs. These 'sick bags', he complained, 'can only encourage those strange people who think that a theatre is just the place for a picnic or a packed supper'. 'How unfavourably,' he concluded, 'the Theatre Royal is now compared with a state theatre in a German city.'

Barnett could not have expected the ferocity, and, indeed, rudeness, of Condon's detailed response. With regard to the music, Condon wrote:

> canned music - Mr Barnett surprises me! Does he never listen to records? Is he too old to remember the benefits of soft lights and sweet music to engender a mood of relaxation and acquiescence? Even eminent historians cannot be that old

His conclusion pulled no punches:

> The writer expects to be allowed to live in a balloon with the now well-pummelled tax payer providing the air of pseudo-sophistication in which Corelli Barnett obviously wallows … I can not and do not intend to pander to pseudo-sophisticates.

He then went on to say that the old Theatre Royal for which Barnett pined 'lacked any atmosphere of a theatrical kind' with its 'clinical appearance … totally unsuited to the image of theatre'.

Barnett, in a follow-up letter, took Condon to task for his poor understanding of language in using the term pseudo-sophisticate (a meaningless compound word since 'pseudo' and 'sophist' meant essentially the same thing). He proclaimed that Condon's 'random personal rudeness … can hardly raise him in our esteem as a person fit to discharge a high civic trust … he regards the theatre as his own personal property rather than as a trust for the city'.

Condon responded with even more sarcasm and rudeness:

> I must apologise to Corelli Barnett; he really must be totally unsophisticated if he … cannot understand my term pseudo-sophisticate … [I]f he means by rudeness that my letter carried sufficient conviction to remove the cobwebs from his Rip Van Winkle world then my writing has not been in vain. As an eminent historian, Mr Barnett should know better than to distort facts.

He went on in slightly more measured terms to set out his philosophy:

> Let me state my aim, and I believe the aim of those who employ me; to attract more people to attend the Theatre Royal for every production. I accept that I may tread on the toes of people who feel the theatre should be for the leisured few, but I would not feel justified in accepting my remuneration if I were to fail to lay before the widest possible range of public the best possible attractions.

That his methods were justified, he continued, was borne out by the attendances, which during the autumn of 1972 were 50 per cent higher than they had been a year earlier. In a final, no doubt intentionally-unsophisticated outburst, he concluded: 'So get with it folks, join the trend of live theatre now!'

Recalling Condon's arrival in Norwich and his fights with his opponents, the *Dublin Evening Herald* recorded that Condon:

> quickly realised what was wrong; the Theatre Royal was catering almost entirely for a certain section of citizens, the well-shod ones, with brows uplifted…The Irishman decided to change that image. He brightened up the grey exterior with posters, photographs and lights, despite opposition from some of the toffee-nosed citizens.[142]

Despite the many feathers he ruffled, Condon soon won the respect of the city and the entertainment industry. Some six months after his appointment, the local paper noted:

> In its day, the Theatre Royal has passed through some dismal patches but now, under the Theatre Royal Trust, with its lively new management, it is a place of enterprise, drive and experiment.[143]

A couple of months later, the industry paper, *The Stage,* under the headline 'Heartening Story of Development at Norwich Royal', reported that Condon's:

> Drive and infectious enthusiasm were apparent from the outset. His energy and flair for utilizing every possible means of publicity are both expanding factors; he rarely seems to miss a trick.[144]

By the end of 1973, it was clear that Condon had succeeded in setting up a virtuous circle. The increase in audience numbers allowed the theatre to book more attractive touring groups, which further increased audience numbers. Condon reflected on his success:

> It was a battle royal when I came to get quality shows to come…[P]eople are now fighting to come here, falling over themselves … Norwich has become a living, throbbing heart centre of show business, and our facilities are the best in Britain … I'm very glad that we've broken down the prejudices. I think the class barrier of several years ago has gone. It's now recognised that the theatre's for everybody.[145]

Three days earlier he had set out his high ambitions for the future:

> There is still a lot more to be done in building audiences and the theatre to a pinnacle completely beyond the reach of any other provincial theatre in Britain. But even now, Norwich Theatre Royal is undoubtedly at the top of the league in the first division.[146]

In the summer of 1974, Condon announced that profits for the past financial year had risen by about 50 per cent and that box office receipts had been broken for the third time in recent months with Ray Cooney's farce *There Goes the Bride.* Condon's success was winning him a national reputation and many journalists and theatre administrators made the trip to Norwich to consult this charismatic and 'chutzpah-laden individual'.[147] What made him a controversial - and, therefore, newsworthy figure - was his view that subsidies rather than providing theatres a lifeline were, in fact, destroying them. In *Municipal Entertainment* in September 1974, he wrote:

> Subsidy in any form is abhorrent to me. Subsidy breeds inefficiency, red tape, jobs for the boys, unnecessary record keeping, constipated systems and a lack of initiative… [148]

New Society carried an article on Condon's 'Norfolk miracle' in which he was quoted as saying that Arts Council grants fossilised theatres as expensive mausoleums and that you don't learn to run a theatre at a polytechnic 'but by "mitching" off school to dig, hawk and sell potatoes to raise money to go the circus.'[149] He was even more graphic in *The Guardian* the following year:

> Sure now, the way they use subsidy here it's like putting the nosebag on the wrong side of the horse. It does the animal no good at all and you end with a bag full of horse manure…

Criticism of the Arts Council was a recurring theme in Condon's speeches and interviews. In 1978, he told Joan Bakewell:

> If you have a diseased limb you chop it off. But if you have a diseased theatre they want you to throw money at it! Fifty years ago, there were 319 major theatres in the country, now there are twelve. The Arts Council is helping to eradicate the theatre.[150]

He was back on the attack in 1981 when he told a television audience that the incentive in theatre was to fail, because that was what you had to do to get the government handouts.[151] Predictably, comments such as this irritated the Arts Council, which saw itself as the object of Condon's 'personalised vendetta'.[152] When questioned once about his disrespectful approach to fellow managers and senior people in the theatre world, he replied that no progress could be made if 'free speech is impeded by matters of status'.

Condon, of course, did benefit from subsidies from his local council. He brought in national touring groups that depended on subsidies for their existence. When pressed on this matter, he would concede that subsidies could be good as long as they targeted theatrical growth and expansion and were not wasted on those he often dismissed as 'cultural masturbationists' in their solitary and unproductive activity. Russ Allen (of The Actors' Company) braved being placed in this group by attacking Condon for specialising in the 'instant audience':

> Take the theatre, add red-hot dayglo posters and lo! an audience. But it is an audience that has not 'chosen' that particular product - it has merely chosen to come to the theatre.

In response to such critics, Condon used to explain that he was not against putting on classical plays, but that his prime concern was making sure seats got sold: 'It is essential to trap the animals before you can teach them tricks.'[153] He admired the work of Samuel Beckett, he said on one occasion, but to put one of his plays on in a 1274-seat theatre would be financial suicide. Condon claimed he had a sixth sense about what would succeed at the theatre and was always prepared to take a gamble on his intuitions. (His critics, he joked, believed that the sixth sense was the only sense he did have.) One of his intuitions in 1976 was to present *Pyjama Tops*, a play that included a scene with glamorous nudes in a glass-sided swimming pool. This provoked the following poetic comment:

For Filling Auditori-ums
There's none like Dick to beat the drums
When classics fail he doesn't fret
A naked bum's a better bet[154]

The poem was right. During this period, the inclusion of the occasional sex comedy in the year's programme generally helped to swell the budget. When the (then) famous nude model, Fiona Richmond, appeared in *Yes, We Have No Pyjamas* in 1979, a new record of 9947 seats were sold - the sales spurred on, perhaps, by the outraged letters in the local press. Sales were helped by the fact that these shows brought in not only the modern equivalent of the Victorian gallery audience but also many of the same people that had already booked their seats for the next opera performances. As Condon remarked, the high- and the low-brow have a funny way of meeting. By the end of 1977, things were going so well that the local paper concluded:

The Theatre Royal Norwich is now so synonymous with success that almost any commentary or report on its activities is liable to seem either bland or overgiven to superlatives.

His successes were not limited to the main stage of the theatre. In 1975, he set up a junior theatre workshop in connection with the local College of Education at Keswick Hall. And in 1977, he transformed the dingy church hall opposite the stagedoor (a former rehearsal room) into a 200-seater studio theatre. It was intended as a venue for local amateur groups and light entertainment (from puppetry to cabaret) as well as classical and fringe theatre.[155] Some years later, Condon introduced theatre arts courses, which (in 1989) enrolled 377 adults and 899 children.

Things continued to go well into the 1980s. About £200,000 was spent on improvements in 1980. Attendances remained high and by 1983 Condon had amassed the sum of £472,000 for theatre reserves.[156] In 1984, Sir Alex Alexander, who had been an independent and effective chairman of the Norwich Theatre Royal Trust and a firm supporter of Condon, announced his resignation. With his departure, the trust board expanded to include more representatives from Norwich City Council and Norfolk County Council. What Condon and others feared was that their inclusion on the board would bring local political issues into account when deciding on theatre policies. Patricia Hollis, the Labour leader of Norwich City Council, assured doubters that the city council wanted the Theatre Royal to stay independent, but Condon remained sceptical.[157] At first, relations between Condon and the trust went reasonably well. In his statement at the 1985 annual general meeting, the trust chairman, Geoffrey Marshall, gave thanks 'especially to our exuberant, energetic, and talented general manager'.

Having achieved his first goals in Norwich, Condon spread his interests further afield through his company Dick Condon Management Limited. He began producing more shows at other theatres round the country and got involved in the local summer season, end-of-the-pier, seaside shows at Cromer and Great Yarmouth. (Condon must have had a particular emotional attachment to the small theatre on Cromer Pier, because more than one performer there has reported seeing his ghost beside them on the stage!)[158]

Colleagues celebrate with Condon his Honorary Degree from the University of East Anglia

Condon and the D'Oyly Carte Company

The D'Oyly Carte Company, a prestigious household name, had since 1875 performed the works of Gilbert and Sullivan at the Savoy Theatre in London and in theatres across the United Kingdom and around the world. As touring and production costs soared in the 1970s, the company grew increasingly dependent on grants to keep it going. When the Arts Council funding dried up, the management launched a *Save the D'Oyly Carte* campaign but alternative financing could not be found and the company disbanded in 1982. Three years later, Dame Bridget D'Oyly Carte, died and left £1 million in her will to help relaunch the company. Dick Condon - who by this time had established a big reputation as a source of advice on how to revivify failing theatres - was offered the post of general manager. He took it on and soon worked his magic. His first coup was persuading Sir Michael Bishop to have his company British Midland Airways provide major long-term sponsorship funding. By 1988, the company was reformed and touring to much acclaim with a new version of *Iolanthe* and *The Yeomen of the Guard*.

In 1986, Condon accepted a major challenge that frequently took him out of the city. On 1 January 1987, he passed over the day-to-day running of the Theatre Royal to the newly-appointed deputy general manager, Anna Claire Martin, and concentrated his efforts on breathing life back into the D'Oyly Carte Opera Company.[159]

With the D'Oyly Carte 'mission accomplished', he turned his attention back to the Theatre Royal. More refurbishment was obviously needed. The kitchens, carpets and toilets as well as the safety curtain and some of the backstage equipment were showing signs of terminal aging. Long famed for bringing top-quality companies to Norwich at low prices, he was finding it increasingly difficult because of the theatre's inadequate backstage facilities. The London Festival Ballet and the National Theatre, in particular, had complained of the space restraints. And Glyndebourne Touring Opera, which had once started its tours in Norwich, now finished them there so it could adjust its scenery to fit the space available. As other provincial theatres made structural improvements, it became clear that unless the Theatre Royal followed suit it would drop back into the second tier of venues. In other words, if the theatre stood still with its facilities, it would be going backwards.[160] The decision was taken, therefore, in 1989 to make an appeal for funds to undertake a major renovation plan.[161] Thus began two years of bitter fighting, acrimony and confusion that almost killed the theatre.

It would take too much time to weigh objectively all the accusations and counter-accusations that occupied those two difficult years. At the heart of the problem were the fundamental differences of opinion and outlook between Dick Condon and his supporters and the trust board. The major issues at stake were threefold: what was the scope of the renovations and how should the tasks be prioritised; when should the work begin and, perhaps, most importantly, who should determine the specifications and choose the contractors. On the first issue, Condon argued for funds to be allocated not only to backstage improvements but also to significant improvements at the front of the house to enhance the comfort of the theatre's patrons. The trust board, in contrast, felt that, since the amount of funds it was likely to raise would be limited, it would be better channelling them into making backstage improvements that were essential to attract back the biggest (and potentially most profitable) touring companies. Improvements to the auditorium could wait for a next phase of improvements. Condon summed it up thus:

> They [the Trust] saw the backstage being the be all and end all. It isn't. The place where the public puts their bums is the be all and end all.[162]

On the second issue, Condon wanted work to start quickly and to limit the period when the theatre would be dark. The trust wanted to proceed more cautiously, delaying the renovation until the financing could be safely guaranteed.

On the third issue, Condon wanted the board to allow him to work directly with a local architect. The trust felt that rather than simply rubber-stamp Condon's ideas, it should seek and follow the decisions of expert consultants based in London. (Condon frequently railed that the money spent on these reports could have been better devoted to the building work.)

Condon also saw the conflict as an example of the city council reneging on an undertaking that the trust would be an independent board. It all dated back to the changes of 1984 when the trust board was expanded to include more local councillors. Since then, he argued:

> Political levels of involvement have continued to take their toll, and it was inevitable that sooner or later a situation as has now developed would arise.

The controversy reached the national press. In the height of the crisis, Joan Bakewell in *The Sunday Times* recalled how the Theatre Royal had a reputation for success and profitability and asked why in the world it was now closed. 'How', she asked, 'has this whole mess come about?'[163] Bakewell took Condon's side and summed it up:

> It is in essence a clash between the highly idiosyncratic person (Condon himself) close to the problem and the committee men and women not close enough.

'Condon', she said, 'had run the Theatre Royal effectively as a family business just as Mrs Thatcher's father ran the store in Grantham.' Would Mr Thatcher have liked a committee of local government officials to design and run his grocery business?'

Despite the disagreements between the two sides an appeal for £2.75 million was launched on 4 April 1989. The trust and Condon continued their arguments with Condon not budging from his position that significant improvements for the audience in the auditorium, bars and the foyer were an essential requirement. The meetings with

Condon and Bowhill banned from meetings with the architects

the London-based architects were stormy and, finally, on 21 December, the trust pulled the plug, accused Condon of 'haranguing' the architect and requested him and the theatre's technical manager, Jack Bowhill, not to attend further meetings. It was this request that really pushed the conflict between the two sides beyond the point of no return. Condon was incensed that their 60 years of combined professional experience were being ignored and that the trust had placed greater faith in a 'university professor and a farmer' to deal with the contractors and consultants. 'The core of the problem', he said, 'is that the project has been in the hands of amateurs.'

Jack Bowhill

Jack Bowhill played a major role in the success of the Theatre Royal during the Condon years. He joined the theatre as an electrician in the 1950s, quickly made himself indispensable and progressed to become the theatre's technical director. He was the one who converted Dick Condon's ideas and visions into practical reality. Yvonne Marsh, who directed pantomimes at the Theatre Royal during the 1970s and 80s, recalled a typical example. She and Condon had made ambitious plans for an on-stage waterfall for their production of *Babes in the Wood*. But building it proved very difficult. About 1 o'clock in the morning she left the theatre despondent and not sure that it would be completed on time or in the way she wanted. She returned in the morning at 8 o'clock to find the waterfall fully functioning. Bowhill had 'worked his magic'. He had stayed on through the night to crack the problems and get it ready. Bowhill's friendly efficiency was one of the elements that attracted many companies to come to Norwich. It was for this reason that Condon insisted on having him at his side during discussions on the renovations.

The trust decided to push back the starting date for the work to 1991. The appeal had not proved as successful as hoped and by December 1989 it had only raised £1.6 million. Trust members thought it was better to wait until the goal had been reached or was closer to achievement. Condon disagreed. He felt that the dilapidated state of the building had to be tackled as soon as possible and was worried that taking away the sense of urgency for the appeal might cause it to lose out to increasing competition for funds from appeals pending for the Norwich Playhouse and for developments in Ipswich.[164]

The arguments continued into the new year of 1990. Frustrated at the way things were going, Condon handed in his resignation on 6 March. The trust refused to accept it and, reluctantly, agreed to begin work within weeks. It also agreed to Condon's request to run a summer season of plays under a big circus marquee in Earlham Park to be known as Theatrerama. The theatre closed on 31 March and work began on 11 April. But all was not well. The appeal was flagging and the public grew aware of the embarrassing arguments between Condon and the trust. Rumours, counter-rumours, allegations and counter-allegations, found their way into the press. Even though many were unfounded, they did much to ensure that the rift could not be healed.

One important element of the dispute was that Condon had badly misjudged the financial viability of Theatrerama. The cost of the marquee soared above original estimates as unforeseen health-and-safety requirements had to be met, for example, regarding the numbers of toilets (and associated mains water and sewerage services) and disabled access. Attendances during a world cup summer were also lower than anticipated. As the season drew to a close it was clear the project was going to lose at least £350,000. It was a large chunk of the appeal fund.

A second (and most important) element was that work on the Theatre Royal building (which had begun in April) had ground to a halt after only a few weeks as it became clear that there was insufficient funding to continue. Workmen had already demolished 20 feet of the fly-tower. There was not enough money to finish the job and replace it or even put it back to how it was; the building could no longer function as a theatre. Condon resubmitted his resignation and this time it was accepted. He agreed, however, to stay on until the end of the September Theatrerama season and to keep his resignation secret until July.

Throughout that summer, with the theatre closed and no work in progress, local people wondered what was going on. When Condon's resignation was announced in July, the discord broke out into the open with each side vying for popular support. Condon explained that he had had no alternative to resignation:

> My views were swept aside and I made it known that when these issues became public questions I would not hesitate to say publicly what I believed to be the truth about the project and the way it was being handled.

He was backed up by his staff. Jack Bowhill, the stage manager dismissed the Trust as businessmen who 'just don't know the theatre'. He observed:

> I have had over 30 years of association with the theatre and I know what it would have been like without Dick Condon. For the Board to have allowed this to happen I find unbelievable. He has given the theatre his all.[165]

The trust chairman placed on record his tribute to Dick Condon for his achievements but signalled that it was Condon's desire to get his own way at all costs that led to his resignation:

> He finds the frustrations and delays of working on the edge of the political and demo-cratic process to be intolerable.[166]

Following this exchange, Condon received numerous letters and messages and some newspaper articles exhorting him to rethink his position. Peter Rollins (a member of the trust board) resigned citing 'some sympathy' with Condon. Backed by this strong support, Condon announced:

> It would be wrong of me not to make a genuine gesture to those who feel, as the newspa-pers have commented, that it is the future of the theatre which is now of paramount im-portance.

He said he would stay on as a consultant if the control of the theatre renovations were handed over to an accountant/administrator. On 16 July, the local paper carried the headline: 'I'll Stay Offer by Dick Condon.'[167] The offer was not taken up.

Two days later, the trust chairman, Geoffrey Marshall, wrote that he had followed 'more in sorrow than in anger the largely uninformed criticism we have faced since Dick Condon announced his resignation'. He defended the board on the grounds that it had persuaded Condon to retain his position at the theatre when he was planning to leave for D'Oyly Carte, had pleaded with him earlier that year not to resign and had always acknowledged his remarkable achievements in Norwich and elsewhere. Marshall also revealed that when Condon had been ill in the autumn of 1989, the trust paid for a week's post-hospital convalescence in a Suffolk nursing home. (This incident may have been revealed not so much to accuse Condon of ingratitude but to signal that Condon was ill and imply that his poor health might help to explain what was going on.) Condon responded to this latter point by stating that his week at the health farm had cost £445 and that he had contributed three times more than that from his own pocket to the appeal fund.

The county and the city councils tried to calm the furore before it got out of hand. They had before them an interim consultants' report, delivered on 2 July, which criticised the handling of the Theatre Royal renovation project. Backed by this report and pressured by the rising public disapproval of the trust, the city council with the support of the county council, asked for Marshall's resignation. The local paper - under the heading 'I'll Fight Sacking Says Theatre Chief' - reported that Marshall had turned down two requests to resign. These refusals triggered a press statement from the city authorities saying that the two councils

> will now be initiating formal procedures to secure Mr Marshall's replacement ... so that a fresh start can be made on the revitalisation of the Theatre Royal.[168]

Marshall wanted to stay put as chairman of the trust and to fight what he saw as a personal slur. But he eventually resigned, claiming angrily that he had been made a scapegoat.[169] The chairman of the appeal committee, Gerry McGurk, also resigned in sympathy with him. Condon did not escape the councils' condemnation. In the same press statement, he was criticised for making too many press statements which have confused the situation by putting forward impractical suggestions, and done nothing to generate the increased public support without which the appeal cannot succeed.

An angry summer of accusations and recriminations followed, leaving both local and national observers perplexed.

Theatres in the red are still being cherished. Ours, usually in profit, has been sent into prolonged darkness by circumstances not properly explained and from which important questions arise.[170]

A reporter went into the theatre building early in September and observed sadly that:

The once red seats are now grey with dust, rain has come through temporary roofing and damaged the stage, the dressing rooms are a shambles of demolition.[171]

On the month of Condon's departure, it was clear that he had won the battle for popular support hands down. In the September issue of the *Norfolk Journal*, one writer deplored how Condon's departure had been forced by the actions of others over whom he had no control:

That such a man should leave on such a note is bad enough. That he is also a very ill man at the present time is something which will deeply disturb the thousands who feel they know him as a friend, even if they know him only briefly in the theatre foyer.

The writer then used extraordinarily strong language against the trust, saying that Condon:

has been called the best known and best loved figure in Norfolk public life. That is something which the cabals of Theatre Trust and city and council halls cannot take away from him.[172]

At the last-night performance in the marquee in Earlham Park in September - when the Syd Lawrence Orchestra had taken its final bow - Condon stepped out to address the audience. He told them that the theatre had been crucified. Could confidence be placed in the present trust members to spend £5.6 million wisely? Should they be replaced? A forest of hands went up to support their replacement. Mike Souter (a Radio Norfolk presenter) told the audience: 'we cannot understand what has gone wrong with Britain's most successful theatre' and led loud applause in tribute to Dick Condon.

Different trust members offered their own explanations of why Condon had to leave but they failed to convince. The deputy Labour leader of Norwich City Council (and trust member), Barbara Simpson, defended the trust by saying:

Mr Condon wanted to do things cheaply and we wanted to do them properly so they would last.

This remark must have particularly irritated Condon who, when he accused the trust of being 'less than economical' in the way it spent the appeal money, was not focusing on the quality specifications of the work, but above all, on the amount being splashed out on consultancy reports. If that remark was irritating, he must have been amazed to hear himself characterised as a conservative force holding back the modernising wishes of the trust. Brenda Ferris, a trust member and a Labour councillor, explained:

> We are trying to take the theatre out of a tatty time warp. Some people just seem to want to undermine and denigrate the efforts of the Trust.[173]

The trust held its annual general meeting in the second half of the month and, for the very first time, barred the public from attending it. It explained it's decision on the grounds that 'there will be no matter of any significant public concern' under discussion.

Condon's resignation became effective on 30 September 1990. He left behind a theatre that was 'beached and broken on a sandbank of stillborn plans, failed financial hopes and bitter controversy'.[174] He remained in Norwich and continued to run his consultancy business from his home in Brian Avenue. He also continued to run his fight against the trust. Spurred on by a groundswell of popular support, two petitions signed by more than 5600 people calling for his reinstatement were delivered to the trust. He fought on pugnaciously for the rebirth of the Theatre Royal according to his vision. He told a television interviewer that while theatres were dying round the country, the Theatre Royal was the only one that was being murdered. He started work writing a book with the combative title *Battle Royal – The Rise and Fall of Britain's Most Successful Provincial Theatre*. (It will never be known what he wrote as, on his instructions, the uncompleted manuscript was destroyed after his death.)[175]

The Theatre Royal was in genuine danger of disappearing - probably in as great a danger as it was in 1875 and 1934 - and other ominous dates in its long history. The difficulties caused by the conflict between Condon and the trust were compounded by the enormous loss (almost half-a-million pounds) made by the Theatrerama project in its 12-week run. This loss of money removed any cushion between what the appeal had raised to date and the next phase of the campaign. Fortunately, events of October 1990 pulled the theatre project back from the brink and provided guarded hope for the future. On 22 October, Sir James Cleminson was named as the new chairman of the board. This was a great coup, because Sir James brought with him a wealth of management skills. He was chairman of the British Overseas Trade Board, a member of other government bodies, deputy chairman of the Norwich Union and a director of other companies including Eastern Counties Newspapers (later renamed Archant). He was also a war hero, and a former chairman of the Confederation of British Industry and of the local firm Reckitt & Colman. He brought with him a large network of influential contacts. Near the time of his appointment, Norfolk County Council announced that it had agreed to give £800,000 to the appeal fund.

At first the trust board members believed they would succeed in achieving their aims. On the day after his appointment, Barbara Simpson said:

> perhaps people like Dick Condon will shut up now instead of carping on, which will not help the appeal.[176]

Cleminson, however, gradually set up a new trust board of 11 members, bringing in people with financial, business or theatre experience. Within three months, all 18 members of the old board had resigned. The new board reformulated the plans for the theatre proposing a more ambitious programme. It relaunched the appeal asking for £3.56 million (£1 million more than before). Cleminson urged speedy success in raising the money so that work could start as soon as possible. Condon was pleased by the boldness of the plans and by the professionalism of the new board and threw his weight behind the new chairman. About this time the results of a secret ballot among the Friends of the Theatre Royal were announced: 95 per cent voted to bring Condon back and 74 per cent said they would not renew subscriptions if this did not happen. Condon said he was deeply flattered by the results, but added: 'It's entirely a matter for Sir James to decide. Obviously I'm not in control of the situation.'

Cleminson, who knew how important it was not to alienate Condon, said that he would consider reappointing him and said he believed that Condon recognised what the new trust was 'trying to do is what he would want done'. Condon promised to help Sir James but never came back on the payroll. Asked one time about a formal return, he responded:

> I never discount anything … I would not want to respond to hypothesis. It would be a matter of if there was a suitable proposal and if there was an agreement that I should be invited to go back … I have every confidence that Sir James will lead the theatre to a resurgence and I am more than happy that Sir James wishes me to support his campaign.[177]

One of the main reasons that Condon held back was that he was seriously ill. The theatre critic of the *Eastern Evening News*, Neville Miller, who visited him at his home around this time, explained: 'Condon was so ill, he would seem disorientated as you arrived.' 'Yet', he continued, 'even then he would respond to company, become lucid and make you laugh.' Soon after this Condon returned home to Ireland. He was admitted into a hospice near his family home in County Mayo and died in October just a few days after the Theatre Royal appeal had reached its target figure, but a couple of months before the rebuilding began. His death triggered warm tributes from theatregoers both locally and nationally. A special memorial service was held before a crowded congregation in Norwich Cathedral at the conclusion of which Michael Nicholas, the cathedral's long-serving organist, played a spirited rendition of *There's No Business Like Show Business*. The local paper wrote what a great pity it had been that his 'life ebbed while the theatre went dark amid the shambles of a rejuvenating scheme that went wrong'.[178]

A CITY MOURNS

Condon's death announced, 18 October 1991

This statement was certainly true but, in the end, Condon got his way as, indeed, he had throughout his life. Predictably, he was widely praised for his phenomenal success in transforming the Norwich Theatre Royal but also for his contribution to breathing new life into provincial theatre. Condon had given 18 years of phenomenally long hours to the Theatre Royal. He had done it, he once explained, because theatre was his hobby - he wouldn't have done it for a job. He proved an extremely hard act to follow. In the words of his eventual successor, he was 'irresistible, unfollowable and even piratical in his swashbuckling style'.[179]

Building work began in December 1991 and in May of the following year Sir Ian McKellen performed the traditional 'topping-out' ceremony. A few weeks later, the box office reopened for business and the Theatre Royal was ready to begin new struggles for success in the rapidly-changing theatre world of the 1990s and the early 21st century.

The 'topping-out' ceremony with Sir Ian McKellen second from left

Chapter 9

1992 - 2007: Approaching the 250th Anniversary

The renovations were completed in November 1992 and, in the interior at least, were a great success. The dusky orange and dark-brown colour scheme was replaced by a more modern combination of turquoise, purple and pink while many of the original art-deco features were copied and replaced or brought back to life. And, as Condon intended, there was greater space and comfort for patrons, particularly for the disabled, who now had much better access to the auditorium. Backstage facilities had been expanded and modernised to the point that large-scale touring companies and productions could now be readily accommodated. If concerns remained they were over the exterior of the building that still retained its unexciting façade.

The theatre reopened on 16 November with a concert by the Syd Lawrence Orchestra, the same performers who had closed the old Theatre Royal in its Earlham Park marquee incarnation. The official reopening came a week later with the Royal Shakespeare Company performing *The Comedy of Errors.* The following month Lionel Blair opened in the Christmas pantomime, *Cinderella.*

Overseeing the reopening of the theatre and its first performances was the new manager and chief executive, Peter Wilson. Having beaten off stiff competition from the 60 or so applicants for the post, he took over in February 1992. Wilson brought with him a rich experience of theatre management both administrative and artistic. He had loved the theatre since his childhood and had been active in student productions while at Oxford. After university, he found some professional acting opportunities

Peter Wilson, manager 1992--

Pictures from recent major productions at the Theatre Royal

Clockwise from top left: Tantalus 2001; The History Boys 2006; Miss Saigon 2005; Wagner's *Ring Cycle 1997*

notably playing with Rowan Atkinson in *Beyond a Joke* at the Hampstead Theatre and with Mel Smith and Griff Rhys Jones in plays and revues. He soon took up opportunities to direct and became artistic director of the studio theatre at Chichester Festival Theatre and later an associate director of the Lyric Theatre, Hammersmith. He then moved into the production side of theatre management and by the time he applied for the Norwich job was working as the chief executive of theatrical producers H. M. Tennent. In this role, he remembers dealings with the Norwich Theatre Royal as he tried, unsuccessfully, to negotiate terms for one of his company's productions, *Call Me Miss Birdseye,* with a notoriously hard-bargaining Dick Condon.

Wilson, as everyone else in the theatre world, was aware of the traumas through which the Theatre Royal had been passing. He was, nevertheless, surprised on his arrival to discover just how deeply they had scarred the theatre's staff and administrators. He saw it as his first goal to draw a line under all this, not to get involved in arguments about 'who had been right' and 'who had been wrong' but instead to move the focus sharply to the future and to how all could work together to build a successful theatre in the challenging environment that lay ahead.

The period between Wilson's appointment and the 250th anniversary has been marked by growing successes both in terms of increased audiences and in the quality of the programming. It is, however, too close and rather too short to analyse in an historical way. Perhaps the most useful way of concluding this book is to take a brief look at the Theatre Royal experience today and reflect on how much it has changed since it first opened in 1758. The one thing that has not changed, of course, is its location, which (give or take a few metres) remains the same. People alight from their cars today on exactly the same spot their ancestors alighted from their sedan chairs or horse-drawn carriages 250 years earlier. Predictably, though, most other aspects of the theatre experience have changed dramatically.

Plays and players

In 1758, at least 47 different shows were put on in a five-month season by just one company, the Norwich Company of Comedians. In 2006, during a season that was more than twice as long, the number of shows performed was about one-third less and, with the exception of the pantomime, all were staged by different touring companies. The 1758 programme was put together by the manager with inputs from the resident actors with their choice limited only by availability of scripts. The selection of plays and the frequency with which they performed them depended on their judgments of how many ticket buyers each play would attract - a particularly important consideration when the size of the audience determined the money that would be made by company members on their benefit nights. The Theatre Royal management today has the same motivation to put together a programme that will be attractive to the public, but its options are more limited. Finding a touring company with the right play and the right cast and availability on the right nights is not always easy.

In drawing up the yearly programme, the management first fills in the dates that are standard from year to year. The home-produced pantomime always spans five weeks or so over the Christmas/New Year period; then there are groups that have arrangements to return and perform at the theatre at similar times every year such as the Norfolk and Norwich Operatic Society and Northern Ballet Theatre. Children's shows are arranged for periods around the school holidays and a musical for the early summer. Dates are fixed for the companies with long-term relationships with the theatre such as Glyndebourne Opera and Matthew Bourne's dance company. The rest of the year is then filled up round these fixed points. It is here that the management has to use all of its contacts to find the best options. Sometimes theatre companies contact the theatre offering their services; typical of these are companies putting together a tour of the provinces before a West End opening or following a West End closing. More often, though, the Theatre Royal has to identify available companies and persuade them to come to Norwich in the face of stiff competition from elsewhere. To facilitate this, the Theatre Royal joined up with The Touring Consortium and The Touring Partnership, two groups that bring together the Theatre Royal and other independent, large provincial theatres such as those at Plymouth and Newcastle. These groups can attract companies by offering runs of several weeks at the theatres of the group members. The two groups can also choose directors, actors and play titles and put together their own productions.

Every two or three years the Theatre Royal aims to stage a major event such as the presentation of Wagner's *Ring Cycle* in 1997 and *Miss Saigon* in 2005. Incidentally, *Miss Saigon* demonstrated the way in which advanced technology now available to the theatre allows more spectacular special effects. Many found the computer-generated images of the descending helicopter on the Theatre Royal stage to be more realistic than the more solid helicopter model used in the West End production seen at Drury Lane.

Today's players are also, of course, much changed from their 1758 counterparts. In 1758, acting was all about strong voices, good diction and a declamatory style, qualities that were essential to be heard over what was often a noisy audience. Actors today have a much quieter and more naturalistic acting style and, apart from the occasional rogue mobile phone, do not have to compete with noises from the auditorium. That said, some actors - particularly young ones who have gained their experience mainly on television and film and not on long apprenticeships in old-style repertory companies - are reluctant to act in large venues such as the Theatre Royal where they find difficulty in coping with the demands made on the voice. The life of the touring jobbing actor today can be quite hard, particularly when there is no guarantee of new work after the play has ended its run. However, riding on the train and staying in a comfortable hotel beats pushing a wagon of props from town to town and sleeping on straw beds in noisy, dark and ill-heated inns.

Audiences

What evidence there is suggests that the 18th-century Theatre Royal was rarely full. Most tickets were sold on the day of the performance and when the weather was inclement, audience numbers dropped significantly. As a result, the management had great difficulty predicting audience size and budgeting accordingly. Predicting audience sizes for contemporary theatre is difficult, too, but with increasingly-sophisticated marketing and targeting of likely theatregoers, audiences are steadily growing. In 2005-06, a record 363,648 tickets were sold representing 71 per cent of available capacity. The theatre has a faithful core audience made up largely by the Friends of the Theatre Royal, a group that numbered almost 11,000 in 2006. This dwarfs figures for similar schemes sponsored by other theatres round the country, the average membership of which hovers much closer to the 1000 mark. The Norwich Friends buy about a quarter of all the tickets sold. The annual subscriptions of this army of supporters brought in £226,883 in 2005-06 and when deductions were made for the discounts offered on seats and other theatre products and for the cost of administering the scheme, it still left a net income of around £165,000. This level of annual support - nearly eight times higher than the average generated by other theatres - plays an absolutely vital part in permitting the management to maintain the variety and quality of the annual programme.

The 1758 audiences would have been mostly Norwich residents or those lodging in the city. In the days when people travelled by foot or by horse or horse-drawn transport, the theatre's catchment area was necessarily limited. This was why the company performed only a few months in Norwich and then toured the circuit to Yarmouth, King's Lynn and other such large population centres in East Anglia. The theatre's contemporary audience is drawn from a much larger area. In 2005-06, only about 14 per cent of the audience came from the city of Norwich; by far the greatest number (about 47 per cent) travelled in by car from the surrounding areas of Broadland and south Norfolk.

Contemporary Theatre Royal audiences are certainly quieter and more homogeneous than their 1758 counterparts. People no longer come to the theatre to be seen or to make neighbours laugh at their heckling and banter. Nor are there any social divides between those sitting close to the stage and those sitting upstairs. The typical audience member has probably greyed over the years with about one-third of ticket purchases in 2005-06 made by those over the age of 60. There is no marked 'high-brow/low-brow' divide today. Light musicals do attract more people than opera performances, but quality drama, such as the immensely-successful production of Alan Bennett's *The History Boys* in 2005, tends to attract much larger audiences than lighter comedies and dramas. Popular comedy drama is, in fact, the only genre that consistently struggles to fill more than half of the available seats.

Finances

There are no exact figures to be found but it seems likely that the Georgian Theatre Royal was only sporadically in profit. In the period from the reopening in 1992 to the present day, the theatre has been fairly consistently in profit. In 2005-06, total turnover was over £7 million and the operating profit was £115,000, the tenth consecutive year that the accounts ended up in the black. This is an excellent record considering that the population catchment area for the Norwich theatre is much lower than those for most other regional theatres of similar size. The fact that the 1935 building was based on a cinema design has helped profitability because all the seats are 'sellable'. There is good visibility from every part of the house and even the top row of the circle is close enough to the stage to follow the action and hear what is being said, unlike the top of the gods in some older theatres. The surpluses generated have permitted the theatre not only to continue pursuing its programming objectives but also to expand its work in schools and in the community.

Different shows generate different amounts of income. Some of the more popular ones require the theatre to pay an amount that is guaranteed whatever the level of success at the box office. For most productions, though, the theatre reaches an agreement with the touring company on sharing the profits as well as the risks of any shortfall in revenues. On average, the Theatre Royal retains about 21 per cent of the profits made. The pantomime (a home-grown production) provides the bedrock finance for the rest of the year - as much as 25 per cent of the year's income. The show is performed from 10 to 12 times each week and plays mostly to packed houses: 93 per cent capacity in 2005-06.

Most members of the audience are not traditional theatregoers but people bringing their families to the pantomime for a traditional Christmas treat.

As in 1758, the Theatre Royal receives no subsidies for its day-to-day operations from either national or regional arts councils. It receives just over £90,000 in support from local authorities, vastly less than the more than £500,000 received on average by other provincial theatres. The Theatre Royal management feels that the local authorities' modest amount of support is a great investment, because of the theatre's positive financial impact on the region. In 2005-06, the theatre directly and indirectly injected £16.5 million into the regional economy through supply contracts and wages as well as through spending by the cast and staff of various touring companies and the visitors to the theatre. This represents about £177 spent for every £1 granted by the local authorities.

With the theatre owned by Norwich City Council, it is not driven by a need to maximise profits but simply to remain in the black while presenting a variety of first-class productions at affordable ticket prices. In other words, it can continue to enhance the cultural life of the city by bringing in opera and contemporary dance and serious drama as well as popular musicals and children's shows. There have been offers to purchase the theatre from large theatre chains, but as long as the theatre is able to continue meeting its goals of high-quality programming at modest seat prices, contribute to educational activities in local schools, provide advice and other inputs to local community groups as a 'leader in expertise' and do all this with a balanced budget, it will be hard for potential buyers to convince the Theatre Royal Trust that local theatregoers would be better served under new ownership.

The Norwich Theatre Royal 2007

A year before its 250th anniversary, the Theatre Royal continued as one of the most successful large provincial theatres, but its public spaces were cramped and without natural light and many of its seats had minimal legroom. On the exterior, it was, as Peter Wilson put it, 'the ugliest successful theatre in the UK'. To remedy these problems the theatre closed in the spring of 2007 to undertake a major renovation programme. Improvements included a completely rebuilt modern and coherent façade incorporating a 60-metre long balcony with large windows; a greatly-expanded naturally lit and ventilated foyer; an auditorium boasting larger and ergonomically-designed seats with more legroom; quieter air conditioning and improved acoustics; more bar space and more toilets and easier access to all parts of the theatre for the disabled. These are all changes of which Dick Condon would have heartily approved and of which the theatre's founder, Thomas Ivory, could never have dreamed. The theatre is well set for its next 250 years.

Chapter 10

1758 - 2007: 250 Years of Pantomime

This final chapter takes a look at pantomime at the Theatre Royal and the way it has evolved during the past 250 years. Today, pantomime box office proceeds are the largest and most dependable source of the theatre's income; indeed, they provide an important guarantee of the theatre's financial viability. Fifty thousand people attended the 2006-07 production of *Cinderella* over its five-week run. Although pantomime has slipped out of favour from time to time, it has been the dramatic genre that has pulled in the biggest audiences throughout much of the Theatre Royal's history.

With its traditions of cross-dressing, audience participation and incongruous plots, pantomime is a strange medley of burlesque, musical comedy, dance, music hall and fairy tales all brought together in a script peppered with jokes and allusions written specially for a local audience. It is a uniquely British phenomenon, performed anywhere from village halls to the most prestigious London theatres. The only pantomime performers overseas are British expatriates, for whom the panto is an essential feature of an English Christmas. Pantomimes keep alive national legends and folk tales and play an important part in preserving traditions of the English stage.

The Theatre Royal provides a fascinating case study of how this genre developed and of how, despite recurring predictions of its demise, it has survived and thrived by adapting to changing tastes and fashions.

The origins of pantomime

Pantomime's origins lie in the 16th-century Italian *commedia dell'arte* - with its stock characters Arlecchino, Columbine, Pantalone and others in a fast-moving entertainment of acrobatics, dance, music, satire and comedy. Although its popularity quickly spread throughout continental Europe, it did not arrive in England until the 17th century. Since it arrived from France, where stage dialogue was banned, it was first performed here as a dumb show. Pantomime, as it became known, proved very popular and the London theatres, locked in fierce competition, soon added it to their programmes. It was John Rich of Lincoln's Inn Fields Theatre and later the Theatre Royal, Covent Garden, who standardised the British format and became known as the father of British pantomime. Rich's pantomimes had three basic parts:

- First, the opening, which was based on a classical myth.

- Second, the transformation scene in which the mythical characters were transformed into those of the *commedia dell'arte*.

- Finally, the Harlequinade, a comic chase scene telling the story of Harlequin and Columbine performed in mime with music and much slapstick humour and which had nothing to do with the opening.

The actors in the opening wore costumes and large head masks that signalled what characters they were playing. In the transformation scene, they took off the masks and removed their costumes to reveal themselves as the *commedia dell'arte* characters with their anglicised names of Harlequin, Columbine, Pantaloon and Clown. In the chaotic scenes that followed, Harlequin used his magic bat or 'slapstick' to perform magical tricks such as turning copper into gold, jumping through walls and cutting people in half.

The Harlequinade at the time of John Rich. Harlequin is holding the magic bat or 'slapstick'

As stage technology became more advanced the transformations became more elaborate with scenery flying in from above on wires or transformed by ingenious systems of hinged flaps and turntables.

At the Norwich Theatre Royal - the Georgian and Regency periods

Recognising the audience appeal (and the financial benefits) of the Harlequinade, the early Theatre Royal managers always included at least one pantomime in their annual programme starting with *Harlequin Salamander* in the opening season of 1758. During these early years, the Harlequinade was the true measure of a pantomime's success. Members of the audience were willing to sit through the opening, but it was Harlequin that they had come to see. A playbill advertising the Norwich Theatre Royal's spring pantomime of 1778, *Neck or Nothing or Harlequin's Flight from the Gods*, announced that

> Harlequin will throw himself from the stage to the back of the gallery and from thence return head foremost over the pit to the back part of the stage, as performed at Edinburgh, Exeter and Plymouth with universal applause.[180]

In the 1782 production of *The Election or Harlequin Triumphant with the Bakers in an Uproar*, Mr Follett Junior's Harlequin impressed the audience by leaping into 'a hat box six feet high'. Several months later, when the indisposition of the actor Mr West led to the cancellation of Harlequin's *Comic Dance of Cymon*, the audience rebelled and insisted 'on the dance or their remittance money'.[181] After some delay the management conceded and 'by this accident the audience saw [the next play] *The Fatal Curiosity* gratis.'[182] Two years later, in *Fortunatus or Harlequin's Wishing Cap*, Harlequin was back on form as he flew across the stage from balcony to balcony and 'escaped down his own throat' - unfortunately, no record was left as to how he achieved this.

Pantomimes were generally written fresh (or adapted) each year and reflected the popular news stories of the day. During the early 1800s, influenced by the surge of patriotism during the Napoleonic Wars, themes became more anglicised and English stories and nursery rhymes began to replace the serious classical myths of the opening. *Mother Goose or The Golden Egg* was performed in Norwich in 1808 and *Harlequin Horner or The Christmas Pie,* ten years later. Arguably, this anglicisation contributed to a decline in the status of Harlequin with his obvious continental origins. Although Harlequin remained an essential character and a focus for reviewers, Clown was fast superseding him in popularity. Actors, on the whole, did not approve of this shift away from tradition and the Norwich Company of Comedians made heroic efforts to restore Harlequin to favour. It was an uphill struggle. The exploits of the exotic-sounding Signor Paulo, who stood on his head on the point of a spear in *Jewels Newly Set or Harlequin's Olio,* were not enough to impress a disenchanted audience. Tired of cheap tricks, they were becoming increasingly critical of the poor quality of many pantomimes. In 1828, the *Norfolk Chronicle* complained that *Harlequinade: The Man in the Moon,* had:

> descended to the lowest vault of the Capulets amidst the universal hiss, which such exe-crable trash called forth, in spite of … Ching-Lau-Lauro swallowing his own head. We feel confident that the manager himself must have been as much deceived as the public were disgusted … we can readily enter into his feelings of mortification and regret on the occasion.[183]

The mid-Victorian period

Pantomime audiences revived somewhat during the middle of the century as increasing numbers of people with disposable income looked for entertainment to which they could take their children. When the Norwich-Reedham-Yarmouth railway line opened in 1844 it boosted audiences still further as people from the outlying areas of the city could now consider a trip to the theatre. Pantomime was the natural vehicle to meet the needs of this expanding new market and, in the 1840s and 50s, romantic pantomimes aimed at family audiences became regular and popular fixtures of the Theatre Royal programme. Pantomime continued to evolve during these years. The opening now had dialogue and - in a major departure from tradition - verbal gags, particularly by Clown, were introduced into the Harlequinade.

Pantomimes were now being performed at other Norwich venues and the Theatre Royal was pushed into introducing increasingly-spectacular special effects in order to

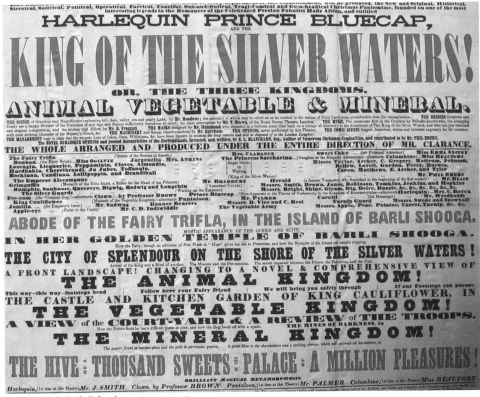

☞IN PREPARATION on a gorgeously novel scale, unprecedented even under this management so famous for its Christmas Presents, an entirely New Grand Comical, Conundromical, Enigmatical, Psuedoiachial, Thrasonical. Demonological Pantomime (Written Expressly for this Theatre by an Author, whose whims, puns, pecu. liarities, mysteries, & Socialities have set every audience in the 3 Kingdoms in a roar)called **RIDDLE** me **RIDDLE** me **REE**, or HARLEQUIN and CONUNDRUM CASTLE, in the production of which, every Artist in the Establishment has been engaged for weeks past, & will be presented in a degree of magnificence and splendour which to be appreciated must be seen on BOXING NIGHT, December 26th.

An advert for the 1851 pantomime

boost its own audiences. This ploy was not without risk and actually spoiled the opening night of the 1848 pantomime, *The Four Naughty Boys, Smith, Brown, Jones and Robinson or Harlequin and the Great Sea Serpent*. In the words of the local paper, 'the machinery was out of sorts'. The Norwich Company had to learn that 'the best pantomime ever constructed depends on strings and flaps and traps and if the machinery doesn't work, the pantomime must fail'.[184]

Scenery and costumes also became important weapons in the competition battle. The 1856 pantomime, *Harlequin Bluebeard or The Fairy Queen of the Night and the Demon of Curiosity*, was advertised with 'new and gorgeous scenery' and series of novel heads by Mr Clarkson of Drury Lane. Bluebeard's entrance was on the back of a magnificent elephant claimed to have been discovered in the immediate neighbourhood

The detailed playbill for the 1852 pantomime

of Norwich. Although the sets could not rival the elaborate and costly sets seen on the London stage, they were, nevertheless, deemed to be 'of a very novel and pleasing description'. The 1858 pantomime, *The Sleeping Beauty in the Wood or Harlequin and the Spiteful Ogress and The Seven Fairy Godmothers from the Realm of Flowers*, was visually even more stunning. The transformation of the Cave of Despair into the Realm of Golden Flowers was 'a gorgeous and dazzling piece of scenic effect' which 'reflected great credit on Mr Sidney the producer who invented it, and the artist who carried out the design'.

The next pantomime was *The Babes in the Wood and Harlequin Wicked Uncle or the Forest Queen of the Fairy Dell complete with Harlequinade*. According to tradition, the story of the babes was based on the lives of two children from Watton, about 25 miles west of Norwich, who were left to die in the near-by Wailing Woods (present-day Wayland Woods) by their cruel uncle. The death of innocent children is not obvious pantomime material, but over the years the story became linked with Robin Hood, who ensured a happy ending by saving the children. The story was reprised in 1878 with *The Children in the Wood or Harlequin Good Humour, the Wicked Uncle and the Good Fairy Birds of the Forest*.

Pantomimes continued to reflect patriotic themes and current events in their plots and it was not uncommon for a scene depicting a new British exploit to be added during the run. Such scenes invariably had nothing to do with the plot. In the 1856 pantomime already mentioned, *Harlequin Bluebeard or The Fairy Queen of the Night and the Demon of Curiosity*, a new scene was added: *The Clown in the Crimea*, with scenery showing a *View of Sebastopol* and *The Taking of Malakoff*. In the 1872 pantomime a scene entitled *The Planting of the Flag in Cyprus* was introduced in recognition of 'our new possession'. Mr Cremlin, who played the part of the wicked uncle in this production, had initially been made up to look like Prime Minister Benjamin Disraeli (Dizzy Ben Dizzy), but the idea was dropped 'so as not to offend the political sensibilities of many of the patrons'. In *Robinson Crusoe and Harlequin Billee Taylor or Man Friday among the Afghans* the following year, reference was made to specific events in the Afghan War while on 14 January, a new scene, *The Storming of Ali Musjid*, was added.

About this time a scheduling change took place. The pantomime had traditionally been performed as the final piece of the evening after the half-price patrons had taken their places, but in order to accommodate the growing number of juveniles, the theatre switched the pantomime to the beginning of the evening. This came as a relief to those more interested in the other parts of the programme, because it meant that the rowdy part of the audience with its loud shouting, singing, orange peel, and ginger-beer bottles left before the main play began.

The lavish spectacle, by now an integral part of pantomime, had a beneficial impact on the local economy. Writing scripts, unpicking and remaking costumes, designing and painting scenery and inventing special effects generated an important industry, which provided work throughout the year for many people. In addition to the professional actors, every pantomime featured a good number of child performers. These were usually recruited locally from poorer families, who were eager to earn a little extra cash. The audience saw the glamour but the young performers had to put up with long and arduous rehearsals.

The late 19th century

In the final decades of the 19th century, the changes of the mid-Victorian years were consolidated. The opening with its comic scenes and songs, its fairy business and ballet had become the main part of the pantomime. The big masks were now only worn by the crowd and those in the processions. The Harlequinade, once the main attraction, was now a mere appendage, retained only because of its history. A pantomime without Harlequin would have seemed a contradiction in terms.

The growing popularity of burlesque and music halls had a significant impact on pantomime. The Theatre Royal, like other theatres in the country, began to incorporate the most popular elements of these genres into its own productions; namely, cross-dressing, revealing costumes and risqué jokes. The reaction of audiences was mixed. They readily accepted and enjoyed the humour of the male dame but the female principal boy played by a mature and shapely woman in a tight-fitting costume was more controversial. The pantomime was a family show and many Victorian parents expressed concerns about the impact that women in revealing costumes might have on their children 'especially at the age when curiosity concerning the forbidden is beginning to display itself'.[185] Such families voted with their feet and, during the 1860s, pantomime audiences began to decline. In 1872, one critic wrote:

> Of late years, the Norwich pantomimes have each been represented on the handbills as 'the best and most gorgeous of the kind ever produced', but in reality when the performance has commenced, they have each sunk the one below the other in public estimation.[186]

While it is true that some people stopped going to pantomime because of what they felt was unacceptable vulgarity, others stopped because they were bored by the old-fashioned Harlequinade and the long rambling scripts. According to the *Norfolk Chronicle*, the 1873 pantomime, *The Babes in the Wood or Harlequin Robin Hood and the Fairies of the Forest,* was 'improved by condensation, but not sufficiently to ensure vitality'. It was deemed a financial disaster and the promoter had to file for bankruptcy. Maybe the pantomime titles during this period could also have been improved by condensation. The longest pantomime title recorded at the Theatre Royal was in 1872: *The Butterfly Queen and the Harlequin King Coccalarum or the Prince Pretty-Pot and the Naughty King of the Beetles who wanted to marry the Beautiful Butterfly.* The 1880 pantomime, *Robinson Crusoe and Harlequin Billee Taylor,* was the last Norwich pantomime to include Harlequin in the title. The following year, for the first time in decades, there was no Christmas pantomime at all. In 1883, there was only one performance of *Little Red Riding Hood* and in 1886 *The Forty Thieves* played for just two nights. The following year, *Goody Two Shoes* was abandoned halfway through its two-week run after the producer, Haldane Crichton, was reported to have absconded with the proceeds of the week. A week later, he responded to the accusations in the *Eastern Daily Press*:

> Sir, referring to the scandalous reports in your paper of my alleged disappearance, I beg to state that I left the town with the knowledge of my manager (not my partner) and the majority of the company, to see my wife who is dangerously ill, and I need hardly say

without a penny of the receipts. I must ask you to give the same publicity to my denial as you did to the original cruel lies.[187]

Pantomime continued to limp on at the Theatre Royal, but for many years it seemed as though it might follow the Harlequinade into obscurity.

1926 to the present day: the pantomime revived

In 1926 the new managers, Jack Gladwin and Joe Collins, recognised a resurgence of interest in the big Christmas pantomime in other provincial theatres and decided that it was time to bring it back to the Theatre Royal. By this time, Harlequin and most of the other elements of the *commedia dell'arte* had been eliminated and the pantomime had become a coherent fairy tale. The transformation scene was retained but as an integral part of the plot. The Victorian additions, notably cross-dressing and celebrity turns, were also retained.

On Boxing Day, 1926, the Theatre Royal opened with *Aladdin* starring Billy Rowland and a London star cast in a format pretty much the same as pantomimes of today. Special trains and buses were laid on 'for the convenience of patrons from outlying districts'. The first night was not a total success. According to the review in the *Eastern Evening News* its 'only' fault was that it suffered from 'a plethora of good things' and lasted for nearly four hours. It was 'judiciously compressed' for the next performance and became a 'stupendous success'. Its run was prolonged by a week to meet the demand for tickets. The *Eastern Evening News* noted that 'pantomime, though nearly moribund in the capital is very much alive in the provinces'.[188] The tradition of the Norwich Theatre Royal's Christmas pantomime had been re-established.

Pantomimes continued throughout the years of the Second World War although directors often had difficulty in putting together a fully professional cast. Maurice King, the stagehand whose wartime memories have been cited earlier, remembers how he grabbed his chance to appear on stage in the 1941 production of *Cinderella*. On the morning of the opening, Mrs Russell, the director, still did not have the back end of the tap-dancing horse. Recognising Maurice - whose mother ran the hotel where she stayed in Norwich - she asked him to play the part. He accepted enthusiastically and found himself paired with a then unknown comedian Bernie Winters, who with his brother, Mike, was appearing in his first professional show. Neither Winters nor Maurice knew how to tap-dance, so they developed a routine where they 'kicked their feet up and made it funny'. Later in the run, Maurice accepted a second role, a man in armour in the haunted-house scene. He loved being on stage and felt quite rich with his regular weekly wages plus the two pounds he was getting for his acting roles.

Pantomimes in this period offered glimpses of Britain at war. In the 1941 production, one reviewer noted how Cinderella ate her 'real, juicy orange…with undisguised satisfaction'[189] and that when she set out for the ball she was accompanied by a fighter escort of flying fairies. In the 1943 pantomime the Dame led the audience in the *Dig for Victory* song and in the same production there was a football match on bicycles between Norwich City FC and the RAF, 'a masterpiece of skill and humour'.[190]

A significant break with tradition occurred in 1959 when, apart from the pantomime season, the Theatre Royal was functioning as a cinema. In the production of *Cinderella*, the popular singer, Jimmy Young, took the principal boy's role. Under the headline *PANTO'S PRINCIPAL BOY IS - A BOY*, the *Eastern Daily Press* noted that

> Gerald Palmer's production of Cinderella at the Theatre Royal, Norwich, banishes the masquerade of the principal boy in tights…Once again it is a case of the ever adaptable pantomime reflecting a current trend … With this innovation, Mr Palmer…may have waved a magic wand over the prospects of pantomime at an uncertain period for live theatre.[191]

The prediction was premature and in the 1970s and 80s Yvonne Marsh, with her shapely figure, long legs and stylish high-heel boots, brought back the glamorous principal boy. After Yvonne, the pendulum swung back to male actors, but the 2007-08 pantomime sees a return of the female principal boy with Nicky Adams appearing as Dick Whittington.

Yvonne Marsh as principal boy

During his period in charge in the 1970s and 80s, Dick Condon and his pantomime director, Yvonne Marsh, were continually on the lookout for special effects and speciality acts. They introduced Aladdin on his flying carpet and in the 1982 production of *Mother Goose* they impressed the audience with a giant waterfall. Pat Adams' dancers, who got a soaking at every performance, were less keen. Condon was aware of the importance of big names in the pantomime and engaged such contemporary stars as Frank Ifield, John Inman, Bernard Bresslaw and Kenneth Connor. He also persuaded Richard Briers to perform his first (and last pantomime) on the Theatre Royal stage.

Much has been said about how British a phenomenon pantomime is, but, in 1983, two American servicemen bought tickets to see *Dick Whittington*. They liked it so much

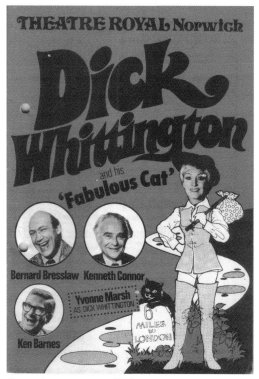

Pantomime programme 1976

Choreography by Pat Adams in Cinderella 1986

that they asked if there could be a special performance for American children from the bases. A Saturday morning matinee was put on for them and it proved a huge success. According to Pat Adams, it was the noisiest audience ever to see a pantomime at the Theatre Royal. The tradition has continued and families from the Lakenheath air base still provide enthusiastic and very noisy audiences.

Since Peter Wilson has taken over the management of the theatre, the pantomime has continued to be the essential feature of the Christmas programme. The actors no longer wear masks and Harlequin no longer takes advantage of Pantaloon but the slapstick and chase scenes of the Harlequinade, the jokes about Ipswich (especially the football club) and many of the Victorian traditions remain. The male dame continues to be one of the best-loved pantomime characters but only

Sherrie Pennington and David Gant with children from the Central School of Dancing and Performing Arts, 2006-07

time will tell if Nicky Adams' *Dick Whittington* has signalled the beginning of a new era of female principal boys.

> An older generation may still sigh it isn't what it used to be, but the truth is that panto never was. It has always reflected what has been popular in show business at the time, for which reason, no doubt, it is still with us.[192]

In recent years, the child performers in the Theatre Royal pantomimes have been recruited from Charlotte Corbett's Central School of Dancing and Performing Arts. Like the child performers of the past, they have to commit to an intensive rehearsal schedule. The work is hard but they throw themselves into it willingly because, for those among them hoping to pursue a career in dancing, it provides a unique occasion to perform with professionals. Inevitably the smaller children are the favourites. They are the ones who get on the most photos and get picked for special cameo appearances. The lucky ones may get a line of their own or be one of those who enter or depart through the trapdoor. All of the children love being recognised by their schoolmates and friends and enjoy the status that comes with being in a show at the Theatre Royal. The cast party on the last night is always exciting - an opportunity to collect autographs and be photographed with the stars. The children cry when it's over, then wipe their eyes and start hoping they will be chosen for the following year.

Richard Gauntlett, writer and director of the Theatre Royal pantomimes, 2002-07

Appendix

A selection of plays performed at the Theatre Royal, Norwich, since 1758

Much can be learned of the historical development of the Theatre Royal in Norwich and, indeed, about the provincial theatre in England by looking at the changes in the plays performed over the years. To help track these changes, this appendix sets out the annual programmes for a sample of five years - the theatre's debut year in 1758 and each 50th anniversary thereafter. In reading these lists a few caveats should be borne in mind:

- the list of plays was put together from newspaper advertising and some extant playbills and may not be complete, nor will it reflect changes to the programme made after the advertising was placed;

- the authors and dates of publication have been derived from separate reference sources, but not all have been found and those dates that were found might not always be precise;

- the lists set out the titles of each play performed, it does not indicate the number of times it was performed during the year. By the early twentieth century, it can be safely assumed that each play was performed every night for a one-week period, most frequently seven performances including the matinée. In the 18th and early 19th century, while the stock-company system was still in place, each play could have been performed just once or a dozen times or more spread out over the year. (Obviously, the longer list of plays in the earlier years reflects the stock company's practice of always including two or more plays on each bill.)

With all that said, the lists are accurate enough to give some clear indication of the way in which overall annual programming has changed over the 250-year period.

The 1758 season

During its very first season at the new theatre, the Norwich Company of Comedians performed mostly comedies. There are fewer farces on the list but most of these were reprised several times, their target audience (those who entered the theatre halfway through the night's programme for half-price) did not mind repetition. *Romeo and Juliet* is in the list of tragedies but it was performed in a version with a happy ending 'for all but Mercutio'. There were some new plays in the repertoire, too, but most were proven favourites first performed more than 20 years before. In fact, the median number of years between the plays' date of writing and its performance during this season in Norwich was 49.

Play	Playwright	Date of writing	Play classification
The Humorist or The Miser Reform'd			
Every Man in His Humour	Ben Jonson	1598	Comedy
Much Ado About Nothing	Shakespeare	1598	Comedy
The Cheats of Scapin	Thomas Otway	1677	Comedy
The Spanish Fryar or The Double Discovery	John Dryden	1680	Comedy
A Duke and No Duke or The Power of Magick	Nahum Tate	1684	Comedy
The Old Batchelor	William Congreve	1693	Comedy
Love for Love	William Congreve	1694	Comedy
The Relapse or Virtue in Danger	Sir John Vanbrugh	1696	Comedy
Love and a Bottle	George Farquhar	1698	Comedy
The Way of the World	William Congreve	1700	Comedy
The Funeral or Grief a la Mode	Sir Richard Steele	1701	Comedy
The Twin Rivals	George Farquhar	1702	Comedy
The Recruiting Officer	George Farquhar	1706	Comedy
The Beaux Stratagem	George Farquhar	1707	Comedy
The Busy Body	Susannah Centlivre	1709	Comedy
The Wonder or A Woman Keeps A Secret	Susannah Centlivre	1715	Comedy
A Bold Stroke for a Wife	Susannah Centlivre	1718	Comedy
The Provok'd Husband or A Journey to London	Sir John Vanbrugh and Colley Cibber	1728	Comedy
The Mock Doctor or the Dumb Lady Cur'd	Henry Fielding	1732	Comedy
The Miser	Henry Fielding	1733	Comedy
The Intriguing Chambermaid	Henry Fielding	1734	Comedy
The Foundling	Edward Moore	1748	Comedy
The Reprisals or The Tars of Old England	Tobias George Smollet	1757	Comedy
King Henry Vth or the Conquest of France by the English	Shakespeare	1598	Drama

Tamerlaine the Great or the Fall of Bajazet Emperor of the Turks	Nicholas Rowe	1702	Drama
The Stage Coach	George Farquhar	1704	Farce
The Devil to Pay or The Wives Metamorphos'd	Charles Coffey	1732	Farce
An Old Man Taught Wisdom or The Virgin Unmasked	Henry Fielding	1735	Farce
Trick upon Trick	Robert Fabian	1735	Farce
Lethe or Esop in the Shades	Mr Garrick with additional scene of Lord Chalkestone	1740	Farce
The Lying Valet	David Garrick	1741	Farce
The Double Disappointment or Shelim O'Blunder			Farce
Damon & Phillida	Henry Carey	1729	Operetta
Harlequin Salamander		1758	Pantomime
The Intrigues of Harlequin and Colombine		1758	Pantomime
The Merchant of Venice	Shakespeare	1596	Tragedy
Romeo and Juliet	Shakespeare	1597	Tragedy
Hamlet	Shakespeare	1600	Tragedy
Macbeth	Shakespeare	1606	Tragedy
All for Love or The World Well Lost	John Dryden	1667	Tragedy
The Mourning Bride	William Congreve	1697	Tragedy
The Fair Penitent	Nicholas Rowe	1703	Tragedy
Agis	John Home	1747	Tragedy
Edward the Black Prince	William Shirley	1750	Tragedy
The Battle of Poictiers	William Shirley	1750	Tragedy
The Gamester	Edward Moore	1753	Tragedy
The Earl of Essex	Henry Jones	1753	Tragedy
Douglas	John Home	1757	Tragedy

The programme for 1808

In its 50th anniversary year, the Theatre Royal's company performed at least 67 different plays. Yet again comedies dominated the programme. The most notable change in 1808 is the drop in the number of farces and comic operas performed and the arrival of the melodrama. Audiences now had more of a taste for emotion-stirring stories such as *Raymond and Agnes or the Bleeding Nun* than for the blander comic musical presentations such as *Summer Amusement or a Trip to Margate* they had been watching 25 years before. The company continued to blend contemporary, classical and old-time popular favourites in their repertoire; the median number of years between the plays' date of writing and their performance during this season was 18 years, down considerably from the 49 years in 1758.

Play	Playwright	Date of writing	Play classification
Tom Thumb	Kane O'Hara	1780	Burlesque
As You Like It	Shakespeare	1600	Comedy
The Beaux Stratagem	George Farquhar	1707	Comedy
The Provoked Husband or A Journey to London	Sir John Vanbrugh and Colley Cibber	1728	Comedy
The Way to Keep Him	Arthur Murphy	1761	Comedy
All in the Wrong	Arthur Murphy	1761	Comedy
The Jealous Wife	George Colman	1761	Comedy
The Brothers	Richard Cumberland	1769	Comedy
The West Indian	Richard Cumberland	1771	Comedy
She Stoops to Conquer or The Mistakes of a Night	Oliver Goldsmith	1773	Comedy
The School for Scandal	Richard Brinsley Sheridan	1777	Comedy
The Belle's Stratagem	Hannah Cowley	1780	Comedy
A Bold Stroke for a Husband	Hannah Cowley	1783	Comedy
I'll Tell You What	Elizabeth Inchbald	1785	Comedy
The Midnight Hour	Translated by Elizabeth Inchbald	1787	Comedy
The Young Quaker	John O'Keefe	1788	Comedy
A Cure for the Heartache	Thomas Morton	1797	Comedy
Secrets Worth Knowing	Thomas Morton	1798	Comedy
The Poor Gentleman	George Colman	1801	Comedy
The School for Prejudice	Thomas Dibdin and Elizabeth Inchbald	1801	Comedy
Town and Country	Thomas Morton	1805	Comedy
Time's a Tell Tale	Henry Siddons and others	1807	Comedy
Begone Dull Care or How Will it End	Frederick Reynolds and George Colman	1808	Comedy
He Would Be a Sailor	Christopher Hazlewood		Comedy
Such Things Are			Comedy
Oscar and Malvina	William Reeve	1791	Drama
Richard Coeur de Lion	John Burgoyne	1806	Drama
The Forty Thieves	Richard Brinsley Sheridan	1806	Drama
Adrian and Orrila or A Mother's Vengeance	William Dimond	1806	Drama
The Wanderer or The Rights of Hospitality	Charles Kemble and August von Kotzebue	1808	Drama

Joanna of Montfaucon	Richard Cumberland	1808	Drama
Peter the Great or The Wooden Walls			Musical drama
The Count of Barbonne			Drama
Harvest Home	Mr Bennet of the Norwich Company of Comedians		Entertainment
The Wedding Ring	Charles Dibdin	1773	Farce
The Agreeable Surprise	John O'Keefe	1781	Farce
Rosina	Frances Brooke	1783	Farce
Animal Magnetism	Elizabeth Inchbald	1788	Farce
Bannian Day	Samuel Arnold and George Brewer	1796	Farce
Too Many Cooks	Matthew King	1805	Farce
Catch Him Who Can	Theodore Hook	1805	Farce
Who Wins or The Widow's Choice	Henry Condell	1808	Farce
The Young Hussar or Love and Mercy	William Dimond	1808	Farce
The Toy Shop	Robert Dodsley	1735	Interlude
King Arthur or The British Worthy	Henry Purcell and John Dryden	1697	Masque
The Touchstone of Truth or Harlequin Traveller	Charles Dibdin	1779	Melodrama
Raymond and Agnes or the Bleeding Nun	H.W. Grosette	1797	Melodrama
Valentine and Orson	Thomas Dibdin	1804	Melodrama
Rugantino or The Bravo of Venice	M. G. Lewis	1806	Melodrama
Tekeli or The Siege of Montgatz	Theodore Hook	1806	Melodrama
Ella Rosenberg	James Kenney	1807	Melodrama
The Blind Boy	James Kenney	1807	Melodrama
The Wood Daemon or The Clock has Struck	Matthew Lewis	1807	Melodrama
The Fortress	Theodore Hook	1807	Melodrama
Harlequin's Invasion or The Tailor Without a Head			Melodrama
The English Fleet in the Year 1342	John Braham	1803	Opera
Mother Goose or The Golden Egg	Pantomime	1808	Pantomime
Harlequin's Reflections on Tragedy (with a leap through a hogshead of fire)	Pantomime	1808	Pantomime
Richard III or The Battle of Bosworth Field	Shakespeare	1591	Tragedy
Romeo and Juliet	Shakespeare	1597	Tragedy
Coriolanus	Shakespeare	1607	Tragedy
Alexander the Great or the Rival Queens	Nathaniel Lee	1677	Tragedy

Jane Shore	Nicholas Rowe	1714	Tragedy
The Gamester	Edward Moore	1753	Tragedy
Isabella or The Fatal Marriage	David Garrick	1757	Tragedy
Braganza, Prince of Portugal	Robert Jephson	1775	Tragedy
Lord Nelson's Death and Glorious Victory			

The programme for 1858

In its centenary year, the Theatre Royal's company performed 80 different pieces, about a dozen more than in its 50th anniversary season in 1808. Again, there is a varied programme but with an increase in performances of contemporary plays. As a result, of those plays identified, the median number of years between the date of writing and their performance dropped to 16 years. The most-performed author was the then-popular Oxford lawyer-turned-dramatist, Charles Reade. The best known of his plays performed at Norwich this season was *Masks and Faces*, his sentimental comedy about the real-life, 18th-century actress, Peg Woffington.

Play	Playwright	Date of writing	Play classification
Masaniello	Robert Brough	1857	Burlesque
The Ladies' Club	Mark Lemmon	1840	Burletta
Delicate Ground	Charles Dance	1849	Comedy
Masks and Faces	Charles Reade	1852	Comedy
The Lost Husband	Charles Reade	1852	Comedy
Honour Before Titles	Charles Reade	1854	Comedy
Used Up	Dion Boucicault	1844	Comedy
The Lady of Lyons	Edward Bulwer Lytton	1838	Comedy
The Secret Agent	J. Stirling Coyne	1855	Comedy
Faint Heart Never Won Fair Lady	J. R. Planche	1839	Comedy
The Love Chase	James Sheridan Knowles	1837	Comedy
Married Life	John Baldwin Buckstone	1834	Comedy
My Wife's Daughter	John Stirling Coyne	1850	Comedy
She Stoops to Conquer or The Mistakes of a Night	Oliver Goldsmith	1773	Comedy
Woman's Heart	Oliver Shepard Leland	1857	Comedy
A New Way to Pay Old Debts	Philip Massinger	1625	Comedy
The Rivals or A Trip to Bath	Richard Brinsley Sheridan	1775	Comedy

The School for Scandal	Richard Brinsley Sheridan	1777	Comedy
Much Ado about Nothing	Shakespeare	1598	Comedy
Speed the Plough or Farmer's Glory	Thomas Morton	1798	Comedy
Still Waters Run Deep	Tom Taylor	1855	Comedy
The Cricket on the Hearth	Albert Smith	1845	Drama
The Man in the Iron Mask	Alexander Dumas and others	Between 1847 and 1858	Drama
The Stranger	August von Kotzebue	1789	Drama
The Lancers of France or The Discarded Son	Benjamin Webster	1853	Drama
Belphegor the Mountebank	Benjamin Webster and Adolphe d'Ennery	1851	Drama
The King's Rival	Charles Reade with Tom Taylor	1854	Drama
The Marble Heart	Charles Selby	1854	Drama
The Life of an Actress	Dion Boucicault	1855	Drama
Martha Willis, The Servant Maid	Douglas Jerrold	1831	Drama
Love's Sacrifice	George William Lovell	1842	Drama
Like and Unlike	John A. Langford and W. J. Sorrell	1855	Drama
Ben Bolt	John B. Johnstone	1854	Drama
The Flowers of the Forest	John Baldwin Buckstone	1847	Drama
Eustache	John Courtney?	1854	Drama
The Midnight Watch	John Madison Morton	1848	Drama
Fraud and its Victims	John Stirling Coyne	1857	Drama
Ingomar	Maria Lovell	1855	Drama
Michael Erle	Thomas Egerton Wilks	1839	Drama
Catching a Heiress	Charles Selby	1836	Farce
Boots at the Swan	Charles Selby	1842	Farce
Taken In and Done For	Charles Selby	1849	Farce
Hercules, King of Clubs	Frederick Fox Cooper	1836	Farce
Eddystone Elf	George Dibdin Pitt	1833	Farce
Founded on Facts	I. P. Wooler	1848	Farce
The Rough Diamond	J. B. Buckstone	1847	Farce
The Dead Shot	John Buckstone	1830s?	Farce
That Blessed Baby	George J. Moore		Farce
Pauline or The Mysteries of the Abbey Granpre			Melodrama

Pauline Deschapelles [Probably The Lady of Lyons]	Edward Bulwer Lytton	1838	Melodrama
Black-Eyed Susan	Douglas Jerrold	1829	Melodrama
Raymond and Agnes or the Bleeding Nun	H.W. Grosette	1797	Melodrama
The Wreck Ashore	John Baldwin Buckstone	1830	Melodrama
Il Trovatore	Giuseppe Verdi	1853	Opera
The Jewess	Planche	1835	Opera
La Sonnambula	Vicenzo Bellini	1831	Opera
Maritana	William Vincent Wallace words by Edward Fitzball	1845	Opera
The Bohemian Girl	Michael Balfe	1843	Operetta
Sinbad the Sailor or The Princess with the Diamond Eyes, the Fairy Queen of the Silver Waters	Pantomime	1858	Pantomime
A Husband's Vengeance	Edward Geoghegan	1852	Tragedy
Fazio or The Wife's Revenge	Henry Hart Millman?	1817	Tragedy
The Merchant of Venice	Shakespeare	1596	Tragedy
Romeo and Juliet	Shakespeare	1597	Tragedy
Hamlet	Shakespeare	1600	Tragedy
Macbeth	Shakespeare	1606	Tragedy
The Swiss Cottage	Thomas Haynes Bayley	1840	Vaudeville

Marie Jean or The Foundling of Paris
Bridal Ballet and Tableau Vivant of Royal Marriage
The Flower Girl of Marseilles
Civilisation
A Variety of Entertainments
The First Night
Art
Spring and Autumn
The Light Troupe of St James's
The Artist's Wife
Ambition or The Throne and The Tomb
Alvar Coeltro or The Secret Passion

The programme for 1908

In its 150th anniversary year, the Theatre Royal programme contained only two farces and three melodramas - much-reduced numbers from those registered in the previous snapshot years. Another noticeable trend is the continuing increase in the number of serious plays (now representing 42 per cent of the total programme) in relation to comedies. The shift towards the performance of more contemporary works continues with the median number of years between the plays' date of writing and their performance dropping below ten years.

Play	Playwright	Date of writing	Play classification
The Taming of the Shrew	Shakespeare	1596	Comedy
The Merry Wives of Windsor	Shakespeare	1597	Comedy
Twelfth Night	Shakespeare	1600	Comedy
She Stoops to Conquer	Oliver Goldsmith	1773	Comedy
The Lancashire Sailor	Brandon Thomas	1891	Comedy
The Gay Lord Quex	Arthur Wing Pinero	1899	Comedy
Sweet and Twenty	Basil Hood	1901	Comedy
Peter's Mother	Mrs Henry de la Pasture	1905	Comedy
The Belle of Mayfair	Basil Hood and Leslie Stuart	1906	Comedy
His House in Order	Arthur Wing Pinero	1907	Comedy
The Truth	Clyde Fitch	1907	Comedy
Diana of Dobson's	Cicely Hamilton	1908	Comedy
Scrooge			Comedy
Richard III	Shakespeare	1591	Drama
Julius Caesar	Shakespeare	1599	Drama
Jeannie Deans	Christopher Hazlewood	1863	Drama
The Harbour Lights	George R. Sims and Henry Pettitt	1885	Drama
Bootle's Baby	J. Strange Winter	1888	Drama
The Sign of the Cross	Wilson Barrett	1895	Drama
Sherlock Holmes	Arthur Conan Doyle	1897	Drama
(The new) East Lynne	Edmund Gurney	1898	Drama
The Girl from Kay's	Caryll and others	1902	Drama
The Walls of Jericho	Alfred Sutro	1904	Drama
Leah Kleschna	C.M.S. McClellan	1904	Drama
The Prodigal Son	Hall Caine	1904	Drama
Raffles	Eugene Presbrey	1905	Drama
Lights Out or Zapfenstreich	H. Havelock	1905	Drama
The Hypocrites	Henry Arthur Jones	1906	Drama
Miss Hook of Holland	Paul Rubens	1907	Drama
The Mystery of Edwin Drood	J. Comyns Carr	1908	Drama
The Bishop's Candlesticks	Norman McKinnell	1908	Drama - Curtain-raiser

At Duty's Call	Si U. Collins	1908	Drama
The Midnight Wedding	Walter Howard	1912	Drama
A Message from Mars	Richard Ganthony	1913	Drama
A Boy's Proposal			Drama/ playlet
A Woman's Past			Drama
£1000 Reward			Drama
The Bread of the Trelawneys			Drama
Henry of Lancaster			Drama
The Christian			Drama
The King of Crime	Arthur Shirley		Drama
Charley's Aunt	Brandon Thomas	1892	Farce
My Jeweller's Wife			Farce
It's Never too Late to Mend	Charles Reade	1865	Melodrama
A Woman's Revenge	Henry Pettitt	1893	Melodrama
The Fatal Wedding	Theodore Kremer	pre-1902	Melodrama
The Gay Gordons	Seymour Hicks	1907	Musical comedy
Maritana	William Vincent Wallace words by Edward Fitzball	1845	Opera
Il Trovatore	Giuseppe Verdi	1854	Opera
Faust	Charles Gounod	1859	Opera
Carmen	Georges Bizet	1875	Opera
Cavallera Rusticana	Pietro Mascagni	1890	Opera
I Pagliacci	Ruggierro Leoncavallo	1892	Opera
Madame Butterfly	Giacomo Puccini	1904	Opera
The Little Michus	Albert Vanloo and Georges Duval with music by André Messager	1897	Operetta
The Dandy Fifth	George Robert Sims	1898	Operetta
Florodora	Owen Hall and Leslie Stewart	1899	Operetta
The Merry Widow	Franz Lehar	1905	Operetta
The Popple (of Ippleton)	Paul Rubens	1905	Operetta
The Girls of Gottenberg	George Grossmith	1907	Operetta
Little Red Riding Hood	Pantomime	1908	Pantomime
The Merchant of Venice	Shakespeare	1596	Tragedy
Othello	Shakespeare	1603	Tragedy
Macbeth	Shakespeare	1608	Tragedy
The Three Musketeers			

The programme for 1955

This is the programme for the Theatre Royal's 197th anniversary year, the closest year to the 200th anniversary when the theatre was functioning as a cinema. In comparison with the two previous decades, the theatre has moved away significantly from its dependence on variety and revues, down from 29 weeks in 1933 to only two. What is immediately noticeable is the overwhelming predominance of light dramas and comedies. There is no Shakespeare and, with the possible exception of Gilbert and Sullivan's *Iolanthe*, not a single example of classical theatre. The theatre retained a contemporary focus with the median number of years between the shows' dates of writing and dates of performance at six years.

Play	Playwright	Date of writing	Play classification
Sadler's Wells Ballet			Ballet
Circus			Circus
Over the Way	Beresford Egan		Comedy
While Parents Sleep	Anthony Kimmins	1934	Comedy
Seagulls Over Sorrento	Hugh Hastings	1949	Comedy
Friendly Relations	James Liggatt	1952	Comedy
Waiting for Gillian	Ronald Millar	1954	Comedy
Hot Water	Glenn Melvyn		Comedy
Widows are Dangerous	June Garland		Comedy
Lady Look Behind You	John Clevedon		Comedy
First Night	Ralph Timberlake		Comedy
Joy of Living	Frank Vreeland?	1938	Comedy
For Better, For Worse	Arthur Watkin	pre-1954	Comedy
Bed Board and Romance	Harry Jackson?		Comedy
Birthday Honours	Paul Jones		Comedy
Night Must Fall	Emlyn Williams	1935	Drama
Appointment with Death	Agatha Christie	1938	Drama
Ten Little Niggers	Agatha Christie	1943	Drama
Reefer Girl	Lorrain Tier		Drama
Because I am Black	Earl Couttie		Drama
Desire in the Night	Patrick Cargill	1952	Drama
Lilac Time	A.M. Wilner and Heinz Reichart with music by Franz Schubert		Drama/ musical play
Jupiter Laughs	A.J. Cronin	1940	Drama
It's A Boy	Austin Melford	1934	Farce
Reluctant Heroes	Colin Morris	1951	Farce
Honeymoon Beds			Farce

Me and My Girl	Douglas Furber and Noel Gay	1937	Musical Comedy
Love from Judy	Hugh Martin	1952	Musical Comedy
Peter Pan	J.M. Barrie with music by John Crook	1904	Musical Comedy
Let's Make an Opera	Benjamin Britten and Eric Crozier	1949	Opera
Iolanthe	Gilbert and Sullivan	1882	Operetta
Puss in Boots		1955	Pantomime
Robinson Crusoe		1955	Pantomime
The Dancing Years on Ice	Ivor Novello	1955	Musical
Showtime		1955	Variety

Select Bibliography

Archive material
Archant Norfolk (formerly Eastern Counties Newspapers) Archive
- Subject Files

Norfolk Heritage Centre
- Arnall Thomas Fayerman Pamphlets NFK/QC
- Bolingbroke Collection
- Condon Collection
- Norfolk Annals
- *Theatrical Observer* z792 (06) NFK/QC
- Tinkler Collection
- Williams Collection

Norfolk Records Office
- Bolingbroke Papers
- Bostock & Fitt Diaries MC198
- Diary of John Bilby, Hair Cutter & Dresser of 10 St Paul's Street, Norwich MC 27/2, 501X4
- Inventory of Plays 1786
- Ditchell, Anne, Letter to Maria MC115/28: n.d. (*c.* 1790)
- Norfolk Drama Committee, East Anglian theatre: an exhibition devoted to the history of the players and playhouses of Norfolk and Suffolk [held at the] Castle Museum, Norwich, 3rd May-3rd June 1952 -- [Norwich]: Norfolk Drama Committee 1952
- Stephenson Papers
- Theatre Royal Inventories and Valuations 1785-86. MC2197/1 Inventory & Valuation of the scenery at the TR - Dobson. MC2197/2 Mr Bunn's Valuation of Paintings of the Scenes belonging to Theatre Norwich delivered Sepr. 15 1785. MC2197/3 Scenery left in the country. MC2197/4 Catalogue of the Plays & Farces, Comic Operas & Interludes belonging to the Proprietors of the Norwich Theatre. Taken April the 14th 1786 by W. Stevenson. MC2197/5 Ladies' Wardrobe

University of East Anglia Archive
- Branford, Colin W., *Powers of Association: Aspects of Elite Social, Cultural and Political Life in Norwich c. 1680-1760*. UEA Ph.D thesis (October 1993)

- Chandler, David, *Norwich Literature 1788-97: A Critical Survey*. Corpus Christi College Ph.D thesis (Oxford 1997)
- Corfield, Penelope, *The Social & Economic History of Norwich*. Ph.D thesis (London 1976)
- Donovan, Rob, *Drink in Victorian Norwich*. UEA Ph.D thesis (2003)
- LeGrice Papers, Theatre Royal Photographs
- Smith, W. David, *Education and Society in Norwich 1800-1870*. UEA Ph.D thesis (1978)
- Tinkler Collection
- Wilkins-Jones, Clive, *Norwich City Library and its Intellectual Milieu*. UEA Ph.D thesis (2000)
- Williams Collection

Publications

Anonymous, *Review in verse of the performers from the Theatre Royal, Norwich, during the season at Lynn of 1802*. n.d.

Bacon, Richard M., *Strictures in Verse on the Performances at the Theatre Royal, Norwich, Towards the Close of the Season 1799 by Norfolk Thespiad*. n.d.

Barker, Kathleen, *The First London Theatre: Materials For A History* (London 1969)

Barker, Kathleen, *The Theatre Royal, Bristol, 1766-1966: Two Centuries Of Stage History* (London 1974)

Bayne, A. D., *A Comprehensive History Of Norwich: Including A Survey Of The City* (London 1869)

Bernard, John, *Retrospections of The Stage* (1830)

Blomefield, Francis, *An Essay towards a Topographical History of the County of Norfolk* (1866)

Brenna, Dwayne, *A Scandalous Affair and a Buried Actor-Manager: Revisionist History and the Life of David Webster Osbaldiston*.
http://www.hichumanities.org/AHproceedings/Dwayne%20Brenna.pdf

Blyth, G.H., *The Norwich Guide* (Norwich 1842)

Boaden, James (ed.), *Memoirs of Mrs Inchbald* (London 1833)

Bolingbroke, Leonard G., 'Pre-Elizabethan Plays & Players in Norfolk'. *Norfolk Archaeology*, XI (1892), 336-39

Booth, Michael R., *Victorian Spectacular Theatre* (London 1981)

Burley, Theodore LeGay, *Playhouses and Players of East Anglia* (Norwich 1928)

Chase, W. & Co, *The Norwich Directory or Gentlemen and Tradesmen's Assistant* (22 March 1783)

Chandler, David, *The Conflict: Hannah Brand and Theatre Politics in the 1790s*. Romanticism on the Net 12 (November 1998)
http://users.ox.ac.uk/~scat0385/bwpconflict.html

Clinton-Baddeley, V.C., *All Right on the Night* (London 1954)

Congreve, Francis Asprey, *Authentic Memoirs of the late Mr Charles Macklin, Comedian* (London 1798)

Davis, Tracy C., *The Economics of the British Stage 1800-1914* (London 2000)

Eshleman, Dorothy H. (ed.), *The Committee books of the Theatre Royal, Norwich, 1768-1825* (Society for Theatre Research, London 1970)

Eshleman, Dorothy H., *Elizabeth Griffith: A Biographical and Critical Study* (Philadelphia 1949)

Evans, John T., *Seventeenth Century Norwich* (Oxford 1979)

Frow, Gerald, *Oh, Yes It Is* (London 1985)

Galloway, David (ed.), *Records of Early English Drama: Norwich 1540-1642* (Toronto 1984)

Gibson, Gail McMurray, *The Theater of Devotion: East Anglian Drama and Society in the Late Middle Ages* (Chicago 1989)

Grice, Elizabeth, *Rogues and Vagabonds* (Lavenham 1977)

Harcourt, Bosworth, *Theatre Royal Norwich: The Chronicles of an Old Playhouse* (Norwich 1903)

Hardy, C.F., *Memories of Norwich & its Inhabitants 50 years ago by a Nonagenarian* (Norwich 1888)

Howard, Valerie, *The Show Must Go On: The Story of the Theatre Royal, Norwich* (Norwich 1977)

Jenkins, Annibel, *I'll Tell You What: The Life Of Elizabeth Inchbald* (Lexington 2003)

Jerningham, Frances, Hon. Lady, *The Jerningham Letters 1780-1843* (1896)

Jewson, C.B., *The Jacobin City* (Glasgow 1975)

Kirkman, James Thomas, *Memoirs of the Life of Charles Macklin* (London 1799)

Le Grice, E. C. (Edward Charles), *New Theatre Royal, Norwich: Its Past History And Present Story* (Norwich n.d.)

Madders, S., *Fletcher's Norwich Handbook* (Norwich 1857)

Mander, Raymond and Joe Mitchenson, *Pantomime* (London 1973)

Martineau, Harriet, *Autobiography.* 2nd edn (1887)

Matthews, Mrs, *Memoirs of Charles Matthews* 1838, 2 vols.

Neville, Sylas, *The diary of Sylas Neville, 1767-1788* edited by Basil Cozens-Hardy (London 1950)

Pinn, D., *Roscius: Or, A Critical Examination Into The Merits Of All The Principal Performers Belonging To The Norwich Theatre For Last Season* (Norwich 1767).

Rawcliffe, Carole and Richard Wilson, *Medieval Norwich* (London 2004)

Rawcliffe, Carole and Richard Wilson, *Norwich since 1550* (London 2004)

Rosenfeld, Sybil, *Georgian Scene Painters And Scene Painting* (London 1981)

Rosenfeld, Sybil (ed.), *The Garrick Stage: Theatres And Audience In The Eighteenth Century* (Manchester 1980)

Rosenfeld, Sybil, *Temples of Thespis: Some Private Theatres And Theatricals in England and Wales, 1700-1820* (London 1978)

Rosenfeld, Sybil, *A Short History Of Scene Design In Great Britain* (Oxford 1973)

Rosenfeld, Sybil, *The Theatre Of The London Fairs In The 18th Century* (Cambridge 1960)

Rosenfeld, Sybil, *Foreign Theatrical Companies In Great Britain In The 17th And 18th Centuries* (London 1955)

Rosenfeld, Sybil, *Strolling Players And Drama In The Provinces, 1660-1765* (Cambridge 1939)

Rowell, George and Anthony Jackson, *The Repertory Movement: A History Of Regional Theatre In Britain* (Cambridge 1984)

Russell, Gillian, *The Theatres of War: Performance, Politics & Society 1793-1815* (Oxford 1995)

Shellard, Dominic and Steve Nicholson with Miriam Handley, *The Lord Chamberlain Regrets: A History Of British Theatre Censorship* (London 2004)

Stephenson, Andrew and Jan King (ed.), *A History of the Assembly House Norwich* (Dereham 2004)

Taylor, Richard, *Index Monasticus: Diocese of Norwich* (1821)

Toynbee, William (ed.), *The Diaries of William Charles MacReady* (1912)

Trussler, Simon, *The Cambridge illustrated history of British theatre* (Cambridge 1994)

Wearing, Stanley J., *Beautiful Norfolk Buildings: Sketches And Notes* (Norwich 1960)

Wearing, Stanley J., *Georgian Norwich: its Builders* (Norwich 1926)

Wells, Hilda, *The Maddermarket Theatre: A History Of The Norwich Players* (Norwich c.1992)

Wilson A. E., Christmas *Pantomime: The Story of an English Institution* (London 1934)

Some memoirs of strolling players

Akerby, George, *The Life of Mr James Spiller* (London 1729)

Bernard, John, *Retrospections of the Stage* (1830)

Charke, Charlotte, *A Narrative of The Life of Mrs Charlotte Charke* (London 1755)

Egan, Pierce, *The Life Of An Actor* (London 1826)

Everard, E. C., *Memoirs of an Unfortunate Son of Thespis* (Edinburgh 1818)

Lewes, Charles Lee, *Memoirs of C. L. Lewes* (London 1805)

Mozeen, Thomas, *Young Scarron* (London 1752)

Panglos Peter [pseud.], *Memoirs of Sylvester Daggerwood* (London 1807)

Parker, George, *A View Of Society And Manners* (London 1781)

Ryley, S. W., *The Itinerant* (London 1808-27)

Templeton, William, *The Strolling Player* (London 1802)

Wilkinson, Tate, *Memoirs of his Own Life* (York 1790)

Wilkinson, Tate, *The Wandering Patentee* (York 1795)

Williams, John [pseud. Anthony Pasquin], *Eccentricities of John Edwin* (London 1791)

Notes

1   Bolingbroke, NRO, BOL 1/93
2   Bolingbroke, NRO, BOL 1/93
3   Grice 15
4   Galloway xxxii
5   Grice 13
6   Hopper quoted in Rawcliffe and Wilson 2004 (2) 107
7   Quoted in Rosenfeld 37
8   To the Mayor and Corporation of Bristol, 20 December 1764.
     http://wesley.nnu.edu/john_wesley/letters/1764.htm
9   Rosenfeld 65. The Angel was mainly used for puppet shows and medleys.
10   Quoted in Rosenfeld 65.
11   Watts quoted by Rosenfeld 54.
12   Rosenfeld 63
13   Rosenfeld 64
14   Rosenfeld 65
15   Grice 34
16   Stephenson NRO, MC1694/1-2
17   The investors were: Jeremiah Ives, Charles Buckley, William Crouse, John Gay, J. Mackerell, W. Fleming, Ralph Smyth, Barth. Harwood, Dan. Ganning, Robert Rogers, John Beever, Philip Stannard, Charles Weston, E. DeHague, Nicho. Ganning, Robt. Harvey Jun., John Ives, John Woodrow, H. S. Patteson, James Smith Jun., Jeremiah Ives Jun., John Chambers, N. Boyce, Hubert Hacon Jun., And. Chambers, and Francis Colombine.
18   *Norwich Mercury* 22 October 1757
19   *Norwich Mercury* 17 December 1757
20   Grice 45
21   *Norwich Mercury* 28 January 1758
22   *Norwich Mercury* 28 January 1758
23   *Norwich Mercury* 4 February 1758
24   Bolingbroke 1/93
25   Stephenson Papers.
26   Pinn
27   8 Geo III cap. 28
28   *Norwich Mercury* 12 March 1768

29 The buyers were (with their share number): (3) Sir William Wiseman, (4) Sir Edward Ashley, (5) Sir Harbord Harbord (MP for Norwich), (6) Thos. Sotherton Esqr, (7) Miles Branthwayte Esqr, (8) Mrs Sheen, (9) John Gay Esqr, (10) Charles Weston Esqr, (11) Robt Harvey Esqr, (12) Mr Jeremiah Ives Harvey, (13) Mr Thomas Harvey, (14) Mr William Dewing, (15) Mr John Morphew, (16) Mr James Beevor, (17) Mr William Fell, (18) Mr William Chase, (19) Mr John Smith, (20) Mr Charles Starkey, (21) Mrs Sarah Salter, (22) Mr Thomas Townsend, (23) Mr Joseph Rumball, (24) Mr Robert Parkinson, (25) Mr Fr. Stidley, (26) Mr Thos Gostling, (27) Mr Thomas Dove, (28) Mr Wm. Wilkins, (29) Mr Richard Griffith (the first acting manager of the theatre) and (30) Mr Wm. Henry Crouse.

30 Proposals of William Wilkins for having on lease the Norwich Theatre Royal and other theatres belonging to the circuit January 1799 in Eshleman, Appendix B

31 *Norwich Mercury* 1 October 1801

32 *Norfolk Chronicle* 4 January 1783

33 *Norwich Mercury* 3 January 1778

34 Bernard

35 Anonymous

36 Bernard 126

37 Jerningham Letters, December (10th) 14th [sic] 1784.

38 *Norfolk Chronicle* 11 December 1784

39 Bacon

40 See Chandler 1997

41 Chandler 1998

42 Bacon

43 *Norwich Mercury* 21 March 1801

44 *Norwich Mercury* 28 April 1798

45 Chase

46 *Norwich Mercury*, 2 August 1788

47 The words of Sir Thomas More in his *Life of Richard III.*

48 *Norwich Mercury* 4 September 1788

49 *Norfolk Chronicle* quoted in Burley 33

50 Williams Collection, Norfolk Heritage Centre

51 *Norfolk Chronicle* 5 September 1818

52 *Norfolk Chronicle* 14 September 1818

53 *Norwich Mercury* 29 January 1783

54 *Norwich Mercury* 3 February 1819

55 *Norwich Mercury* 22 February 1825

56 *Norfolk Chronicle* 28 January 1893

57 Quoted in *Norfolk Chronicle* 28 January 1893

58 *Norwich Mercury*, 16 August 1788

59 *Norwich Mercury* 26 December 1775

60 *Norfolk Chronicle* 15 November 1783

61 Fielding, Henry, *Miss Lucy in Town* (1742)

62 *Norfolk Chronicle* 2 June 1821

63 Norfolk Records Office Minor Collections MC115/28: Letter from Anne Ditchell in Norwich to Maria: no date but the paper watermark and handwriting suggest a date around 1790.

[64] *Norwich Mercury* 21 April 1823.

[65] See Clinton-Baddeley, 79, 81

[66] *Norwich Mercury* 22 April 1793

[67] *Norwich Mercury* 20 April 1795

[68] Letter from Mary to Horatio Bolingbroke quoted in Burley 29

[69] *Norfolk Chronicle* 6 February 1823

[70] For a discussion of population figures see Smith 4

[71] William Geary quoted in Smith 9

[72] *Norwich Mercury,* 1 April 1827

[73] *Theatrical Observer* p93 1827

[74] *The Theatrical Observer* p13 1827

[75] *Norwich Mercury* 1 April 1827

[76] *Theatrical Observer* p13 1827

[77] A letter from a 'Friend to Improvement' 11 March 1827 in the *Theatrical Observer* p41 1827

[78] For more on Osbaldiston, see Dwayne Brenna

[79] *Norwich Mercury* quoted in Burley 57

[80] *The Theatrical Observer* No.31, p123, 6 June 1827

[81] Norwich Theatre Royal Inventory 1846, NHC N792

[82] Quoted in Grice 158

[83] *Norfolk Chronicle* 14 August 1830

[84] Grice 138

[85] *Norwich Mercury* 26 September/29 September 1866

[86] *Norwich Mercury* 26 December 1863

[87] *Norfolk Chronicle* 22 March 1858

[88] See Smith, 224

[89] *Norfolk Chronicle* 2 February 1829

[90] *Norfolk Chronicle* 27 April 1833

[91] *Norwich Mercury* 1 April 1867

[92] *Norfolk Chronicle* 2 August 1832

[93] *Norfolk Chronicle* 16 April 1835

[94] *Norwich Mercury* 17 February 1875

[95] Harcourt Bosworth 90

[96] For a description of this tragedy, see
http://www.wearsideonline.com/The_Victoria_Hall_Disaster.html

[97] Burley 9

[98] Letter from W. B. Wilkins to J. M. Robberds NCRO MS4697

[99] *Norfolk Annals* 12 April 1851

[100] *Norwich Mercury* 19 November 1866

[101] *Norfolk Chronicle* 1 April 1848

[102] Harcourt Bosworth 94-96

[103] *Norfolk Chronicle* 8 July 1843

[104] *Norwich Mercury* 6 March 1876

[105] See, for example, letter to the *Norwich Mercury,* December 1875.

[106] *Eastern Daily Press* 25 November 1920

[107] *Eastern Daily Press* 21 April 1967

[108] Harcourt Bosworth 88

[109] *Daylight* 9 December 1893
[110] Harcourt Bosworth 1
[111] Eastern Counties Newspapers subject file
[112] Williams Collection UEA Archive
[113] Eastern Counties Newspapers subject file
[114] NCRO MC 198
[115] Eastern Counties Newspapers subject file
[116] *Eastern Daily Press* January 1905
[117] George, Ethel and Carole and Michael Blackwell, *The Seventeenth Child*, Larks Press 2006.
[118] *Eastern Evening News* 14 August 1995
[119] Recalled by Maurice King. Interviews with the authors 2006
[120] Eastern Counties Newspapers subject file
[121] 'Pantomime at the Theatre Royal, *Tabs,* March 1971
[122] *Eastern Daily Press* 22 March 1939
[123] *Eastern Daily Press* 8 February 1940
[124] Eastern Counties Newspapers subject file
[125] Interview with the authors, 3 April 2007
[126] Interviews with the authors 2006
[127] *Eastern Evening News* 28 July 1957
[128] *Eastern Daily Press* 27 October 1960
[129] *Eastern Evening News* 1 April 1958
[130] *Eastern Evening News* 6 March 1959
[131] *Eastern Evening News* 15 November 1966
[132] *Eastern Daily Press* 4 September 1968
[133] *Eastern Evening News* 3 December 1969
[134] *Eastern Evening News* 16 February 1971
[135] *Eastern Evening News* 19 February 1971
[136] *TV Times* 14 October 1976
[137] *Illustrated London News*, vol. 266, no. 6964, November 1978
[138] *The Guardian* 24 June 1975
[139] *The Guardian* 24 June 1975
[140] Interview with Neville Miller, 31 July 2007
[141] *Eastern Evening News* 23 November 1973
[142] *Dublin Evening Herald* 24 November 1973
[143] *Eastern Evening News* 1 February 1973
[144] *The Stage* 12 April 1973
[145] *Eastern Evening News* 23 November 1973
[146] *Eastern Evening News* 20 November 1973
[147] *The Guardian* 24 June 1975
[148] *Municipal Entertainment* September 1974
[149] *New Society* 31 October 1974
[150] *Illustrated London News*, vol. 266, no. 6964, November 1978
[151] *Eastern Evening News* 15 April 1981
[152] *Eastern Daily Press* 29 December 1977
[153] *The Stage* 19 December 1970
[154] Williams

155   *Eastern Evening News* 9 April 1977

156   *Eastern Daily Press* 14 December 1983

157   *Norwich Mercury* 14 December 1984

158   http://www.edp24.co.uk/Content/Features/SpookyNorfolk/asp/NorthNorfolk/Cromer Pier.asp and http://www.paranormaldatabase.com/norfolk/norpages/norfdata.php?pageNum_paradata =2&totalRows_paradata=217

159   *Eastern Evening News* 9 December 1986

160   *Eastern Evening News* 5 March 1987

161   *Eastern Evening News* 4 April 1989

162   *Eastern Daily Press* 18 September 1990

163   *The Sunday Times* 2 September 1990

164   *Eastern Evening News* 18 September 1991

165   *Eastern Evening News* 11 July 1990

166   *Eastern Evening News* 12 July 1990

167   *Eastern Evening News* 16 July 1990

168   *Eastern Daily Press* 21 July 1990

169   *Eastern Evening News* 26 July 1990

170   *Eastern Daily Press* 3 September 1990

171   *Eastern Daily Press* 15 March 1968

172   *Norfolk Journal* September 1990

173   *Eastern Daily Press* 21 September 1990

174   *Eastern Daily Press* 18 September 1990

175   E-mail to authors from Vivian Wall Morriss, 20 July 2007

176   *Eastern Daily Press* 23 October 1990

177   *Eastern Evening News* 15 October 1991

178   *Eastern Evening News* 25 October 1990

179   *Eastern Evening News* 20 December 1991

180   Williams

181   *Norfolk Chronicle* 11 March, 1783

182   *Norfolk Chronicle* 26 January 1828

183   *Norfolk Chronicle* 26 January 1828

184   Frow 148

185   Wilson 172

186   *Norwich Mercury* 28 December 1872

187   *Eastern Daily Press* 23 April 1887

188   *Eastern Evening News* 28 December 1926

189   *Eastern Daily Press* 27 December 1941

190   *Eastern Daily Press* 28 December 1943

191   *Eastern Daily Press* 28 December 1959

192   *Eastern Daily Press* 28 December 1960

Index